Issues
for Today

3

Fourth Edition

Reading for Today SERIES, BOOK 3

LORRAINE C. SMITH

AND

NANCY NICI MARE

English Language Institute
Queens College
The City University of New York

HEINLE
CENGAGE Learning

Australia • Brazil • Japan • Korea • Mexico • Singapore • Spain • United Kingdom • United States

Reading for Today 3: Issues for Today, Fourth Edition
Lorraine C. Smith, Nancy Nici Mare

Publisher, the Americas, Global, and Dictionaries: Sherrise Roehr

Acquisitions Editor: Thomas Jefferies

Senior Development Editor: Laura Le Dréan

Senior Content Project Manager: Maryellen Killeen

Director of US Marketing: James McDonough

Senior Product Marketing Manager: Katie Kelley

Academic Marketing Manager: Caitlin Driscoll

Director of Global Marketing: Ian Martin

Senior Print Buyer: Betsy Donaghey

Compositor: Pre-PressPMG

Cover and Interior Design: Muse Group

Library of Congress Control Number: 2010923663

ISBN–13: 978-1-111-03357-6

ISBN–10: 1-111-03357-9

Heinle
20 Channel Center Street
Boston, MA 02210
USA

Cengage Learning is a leading provider of customized learning solutions with office locations around the globe, including Singapore, the United Kingdom, Australia, Mexico, Brazil, and Japan. Locate your local office at **www.cengage.com/global**

Cengage Learning products are represented in Canada by Nelson Education, Ltd.

Visit Heinle online at **elt.heinle.com**

Visit our corporate website at **www.cengage.com**

Printed in China
4 5 6 7 15 14 13

To Joseph

CREDITS

CONTENTS

Skills Chart   viii

Preface   xii

Introduction   xv

Acknowledgments   xx

UNIT 1   Trends in Living   1

Chapter 1   **A Cultural Difference: Being on Time**   2

In some cultures, it is important to be on time; however, on time *can have different meanings in different cultures.*

Chapter 2   **Changing Lifestyles and New Eating Habits**   18

The way you live affects the way you eat. Sometimes when people change their lifestyles, they change their eating habits, too.

Chapter 3   **Technology Competes for Family Time**   36

As computer use and the Internet become more and more popular, families are spending less and less time together.

UNIT 2   Issues in Society   57

Chapter 4   **Language: Is It Always Spoken?**   58

Babies learn to communicate in different ways. For babies who are hearing-impaired, there are other ways to "speak."

Chapter 5   **Loneliness: How Can We Overcome It?**   75

Everyone feels lonely sometimes. However, for some people, loneliness can last a long time. This can be very dangerous to their health.

Chapter 6   **The Importance of Grandmothers**   92
*Grandmothers are usually a very happy part
of their grandchildren's lives. They are very
important for other reasons, too.*

UNIT 3   Justice and Crime   117

Chapter 7   **Innocent until Proven Guilty: The Criminal Court System**   118
*The American court system protects the rights
of the people. How does the American court
system work?*

Chapter 8   **The Reliability of Eyewitnesses**   135
*An eyewitness to a crime can be very important
in solving that crime. However, sometimes
even an eyewitness can make a mistake.*

Chapter 9   **Solving Crimes with Modern Technology**   154
*Today, there are many improvements in crime
technology. This modern technology helps
solve crimes faster and better.*

UNIT 4   Science and History   177

Chapter 10   **Ancient Artifacts and Ancient Air**   178
*Archeologists make important discoveries
about people who lived a long time ago. This
knowledge of the past can help us in the future.*

Chapter 11   **Medical Technology: Saving Lives with Robotics**   197
*Modern surgery is becoming safer and taking less
time because doctors have begun using robotic
technology to help them perform operations.*

Chapter 12   **Mars: Our Neighbor in Space**   **213**

*There are some surprising similarities between
the Earth and Mars. Future missions to Mars
may help us answer some interesting questions
about our own planet, too.*

Index of Key Words and Phrases   **233**
Skills Index   **235**

SKILLS

Unit	Chapter and Title	Reading Skills Focus	Structure Focus	Follow-Up Activities Skills Focus
Unit 1 **Trends in Living** *Page 1*	**Chapter 1** **A Cultural Difference: Being on Time** *Page 2*	• Preview reading through title and prereading questions • Understand True/False, Multiple Choice, Short Answer questions • Use context clues to understand and use vocabulary • Identify main ideas and details • Organize information using a flowchart • Use flowchart to recall and summarize information	• Identify and compare parts of speech in context: nouns, verbs, and adjectives • Recognize nouns by the suffixes: *-ing* and *-ation* and use them correctly • Use singular and plural nouns; use affirmative and negative verb forms appropriately in sentences	• *Speaking:* Express opinions supported by examples; predict • *Writing:* Write a journal entry; react personally to a reading; use a graphic organizer to develop ideas
	Chapter 2 **Changing Lifestyles and New Eating Habits** *Page 18*	• Preview reading through title and prereading questions • Understand True/False, Multiple Choice, Short Answer questions • Use context clues to understand and use vocabulary • Identify main ideas and details • Organize information using a flowchart • Use flowchart to recall and summarize information • Read and interpret bar graphs • Make inferences • Assert opinions	• Identify and compare parts of speech in context: nouns, verbs, and adjectives • Recognize the suffixes: *-er* and *-en* and use them correctly • Use singular and plural nouns; use affirmative and negative verb forms appropriately in sentences	• *Listening:* Share information and support opinions by example • *Writing:* Write an explanatory paragraph using description and examples; write a journal entry expressing likes and dislikes; use a graphic organizer to list ideas
	Chapter 3 **Technology Competes for Family Time** *Page 36*	• Preview reading through title and prereading questions • Understand True/False, Multiple Choice, Short Answer questions • Use context clues to understand vocabulary • Identify main ideas and details • Organize information using a flowchart • Use flowchart to recall and summarize information	• Identify parts of speech from context: adjectives, verbs, and nouns • Recognize the suffixes: *-tion* and *-ation* and use them correctly • Use the simple present tense and simple future tense in the positive and the negative	• *Listening:* Share information and support opinions by example • *Writing:* Write a journal entry explaining the positive and negative effects of technology
Unit 2 **Issues in Society** *Page 57*	**Chapter 4** **Language: Is It Always Spoken?** *Page 58*	• Use prereading questions to activate background knowledge • Preview illustration and title to aid comprehension • Understand True/False, Multiple Choice, Short Answer questions • Skim reading for main idea • Scan for information • Use context clues to understand vocabulary • Organize information using an outline • Use outline to recall and summarize information • Choose correct dictionary definitions	• Identify parts of speech in context: nouns and adjectives • Use past, present, or future verb tenses in the affirmative or negative form • Recognize the suffixes: *-ing*, and *-ce* and use them correctly	• *Discussion:* Describe nonverbal communication; research ASL and discuss results • *Writing:* Write a brief biography of a famous person with hearing loss; write a journal entry about learning sign language; list advantages and disadvantages of the choice to remain nonhearing or deaf

Unit	Chapter and Title	Reading Skills Focus	Structure Focus	Follow-Up Activities Skills Focus
	Chapter 5 **Loneliness:** **How Can We** **Overcome It?** *Page 75*	• Use prereading questions to activate background knowledge • Preview visual and title to aid comprehension • Understand True/False, Multiple Choice, Short Answer questions • Use context clues to understand vocabulary • Skim reading for main idea and scan for important details • Organize information using a flowchart • Use flowchart to recall and summarize information • Make inferences • Choose correct dictionary definitions	• Identify parts of speech in context: nouns, adjectives, and verbs • Use singular or plural nouns as required by context • Recognize the suffixes: *-ness* and *-ity* and use them correctly	• *Discussion:* Discuss causes of loneliness and research on the subject; discuss survey result • *Writing:* Write a journal entry about loneliness; take a survey about loneliness
	Chapter 6 **The Importance** **of Grandmothers** *Page 92*	• Use prereading questions to activate background knowledge • Preview title to predict reading topic • Understand True/False, Multiple Choice, Short Answer questions • Skim reading for main idea • Scan for supporting details • Make inferences • Organize information using a flowchart • Use flowchart to recall and summarize information • Use context clues to understand vocabulary • Read and interpret data in pie and bar charts	• Identify parts of speech in context: nouns, verbs, and adjectives • Recognize the suffixes: *-tion* and *-ce* and use them correctly • Use the affirmative or negative of a past, present, or future verb tense • Use singular and plural forms of nouns	• *Discussion:* Make comparisons about grandmothers and discuss reasons for opinions; discuss unit themes and support ideas with examples • *Writing:* Conduct a survey and record answers in a chart; write a journal entry about the treatment of grandchildren
Unit 3 **Justice and Crime** *Page 117*	**Chapter 7** **Innocent until** **Proven Guilty:** **The Criminal** **Court System** *Page 118*	• Preview visuals and title to aid comprehension and predict reading content • Use prereading questions to activate background knowledge • Understand True/False, Multiple Choice, Short Answer questions • Skim reading for main idea • Make inferences • Organize information using a flowchart • Use flowchart to recall and summarize information • Use context clues to understand vocabulary • Choose correct dictionary definitions	• Identify parts of speech in context: nouns, verbs, and adjectives • Recognize the suffixes: *-ment* and *-ity* and use them correctly • Use the affirmative or negative of a past, present, or future verb tense • Use singular and plural forms of nouns	• *Discussion:* Discuss process of arrest in small groups; read different print media about a crime and conduct a trial • *Writing:* Write an opinion journal entry about participating in a jury; compare advantages and disadvantages of justice systems in different countries • *Viewing:* Observe a courtroom trial and report observations to class

SKILLS

Unit	Chapter and Title	Reading Skills Focus	Structure Focus	Follow-Up Activities Skills Focus
	Chapter 8 **The Reliability of Eyewitnesses** *Page 135*	• Preview visuals and title to aid comprehension and predict reading content • Use prereading questions to activate background knowledge • Understand True/False, Multiple Choice, Short Answer questions • Skim reading for main idea • Organize information using an outline • Use outline to recall and summarize information • Use context clues to understand vocabulary • Choose correct dictionary definitions	• Identify parts of speech in context: nouns, adjectives, and prepositions • Recognize the suffixes: -ence and -ance and use them correctly • Use the affirmative or negative of a past, present, or future verb tense • Use singular and plural forms of nouns	• *Discussion:* Discuss famous cases of mistaken identity • *Writing:* Write an opinion paragraph about eyewitness reliability; write a journal entry about witnessing a crime
	Chapter 9 **Solving Crimes with Modern Technology** *Page 154*	• Use prereading questions to activate background knowledge about crime and technology • Understand True/False, Multiple Choice, Short Answer questions • Skim reading for main idea • Scan for important details • Make inferences • Organize information using a chart • Use chart to recall and summarize information • Use context clues to understand vocabulary • Choose correct dictionary definitions • Study visual aids and make comparisons • Read and interpret data in line graphs	• Identify parts of speech in context: nouns and verbs • Recognize the suffix: -ment and use it correctly • Use the affirmative or negative of a past, present, or future verb tense • Use singular and plural forms of nouns	• *Discussion:* Explain your opinion about the reliability of evidence such as fingerprints; discuss topics such as arrest, evidence, eyewitnesses, and crime technology • *Writing:* Make a list of types of crime-solving technology; write a journal entry about technology and crime
Unit 4 **Science and History** *Page 177*	**Chapter 10** **Ancient Artifacts and Ancient Air** *Page 178*	• Use background knowledge to understand reading through prereading questions • Understand True/False, Multiple Choice, Short Answer questions • Scan reading for main idea • Use context clues to understand vocabulary • Take notes and organize information using an outline • Use outline to recall and summarize information • Select accurate dictionary definitions	• Use parts of speech correctly in context: nouns, verbs, adjectives, and conjunctions • Use the affirmative or negative forms of the past, present, and future verb tenses • Recognize the suffixes: -ion, -ation, and -y and use them correctly	• *Discussion:* Discuss issues regarding the discoveries and ethics of archeology • *Writing:* Make plans about a hypothetical archeological situation in a group and compare plans with other groups; write a journal entry about an archeological decision

Unit	Chapter and Title	Reading Skills Focus	Structure Focus	Follow-Up Activities Skills Focus
	Chapter 11 **Medical Technology: Saving Lives with Robotics** *Page 197*	• Preview chapter through title, visuals, and questions • Understand True/False, Multiple Choice, Short Answer questions • Use context clues to understand vocabulary • Scan reading for main ideas • Take notes and organize information using a chart • Use chart to recall and summarize information • Select accurate dictionary definitions	• Use parts of speech correctly in context: nouns, verbs, adjectives, and adverbs • Use the affirmative or negative forms of the past, present, and future verb tenses • Use the singular or plural forms of nouns • Recognize the suffix: *-ment* and use it correctly	• *Discussion:* Discuss the future of medical technology; conduct an interview about medical technology • *Writing:* Write a journal entry about an experience in a hospital; write a description of a medical procedure
	Chapter 12 **Mars: Our Neighbor in Space** *Page 213*	• Preview chapter visuals • Use prereading questions to activate background knowledge and predict topic of reading • Understand True/False, Multiple Choice, Short Answer questions • Use context clues to understand vocabulary • Scan reading for the main idea • Organize information using a flowchart • Use flowchart to recall and summarize information • Choose accurate dictionary definitions	• Identify parts of speech in context: nouns, adjectives, and verbs • Recognize the suffixes: *-ion* and *-ation* and use them correctly • Use singular and plural forms of nouns • Use the affirmative or negative forms of the past, present, and future verb tenses	• *Discussion:* Discuss opinions about extraterrestrial life; compare space programs in different countries; discuss technology and support opinions with examples • *Writing:* Research details about other planets in the solar system; record details on a chart; compare charts with other classmates; write a journal entry on your opinion of whether life exists on other planets

• **Index of Key Words and Phrases** *Page 233*
• **Skills Index** *Page 235*

PREFACE

Issues for Today, Fourth Edition, is a reading skills text intended for intermediate, academically oriented students of English as a second or foreign language (ESL/EFL). The passages in this thematically organized book introduce students to topics of universal interest. As students work with the materials in each chapter, they develop the kinds of extensive and intensive reading skills they will need to achieve academic success in English.

Issues for Today is one in a series of five reading skills texts. The complete series has been designed to meet the needs of students from the beginning to the advanced levels and includes the following:

- *Reading for Today 1: Themes for Today*   beginning
- *Reading for Today 2: Insights for Today*   high beginning
- *Reading for Today 3: Issues for Today*   intermediate
- *Reading for Today 4: Concepts for Today*   high intermediate
- *Reading for Today 5: Topics for Today*   advanced

Issues for Today, Fourth Edition, consists of four thematic units. Each unit contains three chapters that deal with related subjects. Each chapter is independent, entirely separate in content, from the other two chapters contained in that unit. This gives the instructor the option of either completing entire units or choosing individual chapters as a focus in class.

All of the chapters provide students with interesting and stimulating topics to read, think about, discuss, and write about. The initial exercises are an introduction to each reading passage and encourage students to think about the ideas, facts, and vocabulary that will be presented. The exercises that follow the reading passage are intended to improve reading comprehension skills as well as comprehension of English sentence structure. The activities will help them see relationships between parts of a sentence, between sentences, and between and within paragraphs.

The articles contain useful vocabulary that students can use in the real world, and the exercises are designed to sharpen their ability to learn vocabulary from context. Students should learn not to rely on a bilingual dictionary. A Word Form exercise is included in each chapter to help students develop a "feel" for the patterns of word forms in English and an awareness of morphemes; for example, the suffix *-tion* always indicates a noun. Many vocabulary and word form selections are repeated in subsequent chapters to provide reinforcement.

The progression of exercises and activities in each chapter leads students through general comprehension of main ideas, specific information, understanding structural details, and specific vocabulary. Since reading college material also involves note-taking skills, students are trained to organize the information in the readings using tables, flowcharts, and outlines, and to briefly summarize the passages. Finally, students practice manipulating new vocabulary by working with different parts of speech, and varying the tense in both affirmative and negative forms, and singular and plural forms.

New to the Fourth Edition

Issues for Today, Fourth Edition, maintains the effective approach of the third edition with several significant improvements. This enhanced edition takes a more in-depth approach to vocabulary development and application by consistently introducing, practicing, and assessing vocabulary in context, while teaching valuable vocabulary-building skills that are recycled throughout the series.

The new vocabulary development additions include the introduction of new *Vocabulary in Context* sections to every chapter, which reinforce the vocabulary from the reading along with related words and concepts. The *Word Forms* sections now combine sentences into paragraphs to further develop the contextualized approach. Finally, *Word Partnership* boxes have been added from the *Collins COBUILD School Dictionary of American English* to increase students' ability to use language appropriately.

The fourth edition also contains two new chapters with cutting edge topics: "Technology Competes for Family Time" demonstrates how modern technologies make it difficult for families to spend quality time together. "Medical Technology: Saving Lives with Robotics" describes how doctors have begun using robots to perform surgery.

Issues for Today contains an enhanced *Prereading Preparation* section, which provides thoughtful, motivating illustrations and activities. The fourth edition includes improved graphics, art and photos, which are designed to facilitate students' understanding of the text they relate to. For an introduction to academic skills, *Information Organization* exercises include a main idea activity as well as outlines, charts, and flowcharts. This design takes into account students' different learning and organizational styles. For the development of critical thinking skills, the *Critical Thinking Strategies* section challenges students to apply the topic of the chapter to their own lives and draw conclusions.

All of these revisions and enhancements to *Issues for Today, Fourth Edition,* have been designed to help students improve their reading skills, build a stronger vocabulary, develop more interest in and confidence with text as they work through it—and, thus, be better prepared for the realities of academic work and the demands of the technical world.

INTRODUCTION

How to Use This Book

Each chapter in this book consists of the following:

- Prereading Preparation
- Reading Passage
- Fact-Finding Exercise
- Reading Analysis
- Information Organization
- Information Recall and Summary
- Dictionary Skills
- Word Forms
- Vocabulary in Context
- Critical Thinking Strategies
- Topics for Discussion and Writing
- Follow-Up Activities
- Cloze Quiz

Each unit contains a *Unit Crossword Puzzle* which incorporates vocabulary from all three chapters. Each unit ends with a *Unit Discussion* which ties together the related topics of the three chapters. There is an *Index of Key Words and Phrases* at the end of the book.

Prereading Preparation

This prereading activity is designed to stimulate student interest and provide preliminary vocabulary for the reading passage. The importance of prereading preparation should not be underestimated. Studies have shown the positive effect of prereading preparation in motivating students, activating background knowledge, and enhancing reading comprehension. Time should be spent describing and discussing the photographs and illustrations as well as discussing the chapter title and the prereading questions. Furthermore, students should try to relate the topic to their own experiences and predict what they are going to read about.

Reading Passage

Students will read the passage at least two times. They should be instructed to time themselves and to try to aim for a higher reading speed the second time they read the passage. They should also be encouraged to read *ideas,* not just words.

Fact-Finding Exercise

After reading the passage again, students will read the *True/False* statements and check whether they are true or false. If a statement is false, students will rewrite the statement so that it is true. They will then go back to the passage and find the line(s) that contain the correct answer. This activity can be done individually or in groups.

Reading Analysis

Students will read each question and answer it. The first question in this section always refers to the main idea. There are three possible answers. Two answers are incorrect because they are too general or too narrow, they are not mentioned in the passage, or they are false. When going over the exercise, the teacher should discuss with students why the other two answers are incorrect. The rest of this exercise requires students to think about the structure of the sentences and paragraphs, and the relationships of ideas to one another. This exercise is very effective when done in groups. It may also be done individually, but if done in groups it gives students an excellent opportunity to discuss possible answers.

Information Organization

In this exercise, students are asked to read the passage again, take notes, and organize the information they have just read. They may be asked to complete an outline, table, or flowchart. The teacher may want to review the concept of note-taking before beginning the exercise. The outline, table, or flowchart can be sketched on the board by the teacher or a student and completed by individual students in front of the class. Variations can be discussed by the class as a group. It should be pointed out to students that in American colleges, teachers often base their exams on the notes that students are expected to take during class lectures and that they will also be tested on their notes.

Information Recall and Summary

The questions in this exercise are based on the notes students took in the *Information Organization* exercise. Students should be instructed to read the questions and then to refer to their notes to answer them. They are also asked to write a summary of the article. The teacher may want to review how to summarize at the beginning of the class. This section can be prepared in class and discussed. Alternatively, it can be assigned for homework.

Dictionary Skills

The entries in this section have been taken from Heinle's *Newbury House Dictionary of American English* and provide students with practice in using an English-English dictionary, while teaching the appropriate and relevant meanings of unfamiliar words. Students are given dictionary entries for words in the text. A sentence containing the unknown word is provided below each entry. Students read the entry and select the appropriate definition, given the context provided. Students need to understand that this is not always a clear process; some entries are similar. They should be encouraged to carefully read all of the possible definitions in the context in which the word is given, and to consider which meaning makes the most sense. After selecting the appropriate entry, students may read two or three sentences and choose which one conveys the meaning of the definition selected, or they may be asked to rewrite a sentence. Students can work in pairs on this exercise and report back to the class. They should be prepared to justify their choice.

Word Forms

As an introduction to the word form exercises in this book, it is recommended that the teacher first review parts of speech, especially verbs, nouns, adjectives, and adverbs. Teachers should point out each word form's position in a sentence. Students will develop a sense for which part of speech is missing in a given sentence. Teachers should also point out clues to tense and number, and whether an idea is affirmative or negative. Each section has its own instructions, depending on the particular pattern that is being introduced. For example, in the section containing words which take *-tion* in the noun form, the teacher can explain that in this exercise students will look at the verb and noun forms of two types of words that use the suffix *-tion* in their noun form. (1) Some words simply add *-tion* to the verb: sugges*t*/sugges*tion*; if the word ends in *e*, the *e* is dropped first: produc*e*/produc*tion*; (2) other words can drop a final *e* and add *-ation:* examin*e*/examin*ation*. This exercise is very effective when done in pairs because students can discuss their answers. After students have a working knowledge of this type of exercise, it can be assigned for homework. *Word Partnership* boxes selected from the *Collins COBUILD School Dictionary of American English* are used to reinforce and enhance this section. The teacher can use the examples given in the directions for each chapter's *Word Form* section and the words in each *Word Partnership* box at the end of each section to see that students understand the exercise.

Vocabulary in Context

This is a fill-in exercise designed as a review of the items in the previous exercises. This vocabulary has been covered in the *Reading Analysis, Dictionary Skills,* or *Word Forms* exercises. It can be done for homework as a review or in class as group work.

Critical Thinking Strategies

The goal of the exercise is for students to go beyond the reading itself to form their own ideas and opinions on aspects of the topic discussed. Students reflect on the content of the reading and think about the implications of the information they have read. Students can work on these questions as an individual writing exercise or orally as a small-group discussion activity. In this activity, students are encouraged to use the vocabulary they have been learning.

Topics for Discussion and Writing

In this section, students are encouraged to use the information and vocabulary from the passage both orally and in writing. The writing assignment may be done in class or at home. There is a **Write in your journal** suggestion for every chapter. Students should be encouraged to keep a journal and respond to these questions. The teacher may want to read and respond to the students' journal entries, but not correct them.

Follow-Up Activities

This section contains various activities appropriate to the information in the passages. Some activities are designed for pair and small-group work. Students are encouraged to use the information and vocabulary from the passages both orally and in writing. Some activities such as surveys prompt students to interact with native English speakers to collect data in the "real world" which they chart or graph and then discuss in class. For other activity types, teachers may assign certain questions or the entire activity as an at-home or in-class assignment.

Cloze Quiz

The *Cloze Quiz* tests not only vocabulary but also sentence structure and comprehension in general. The quiz is a modified version of the reading passage itself, with 20 items to be completed. At the top of the answer page, students are given the 20 words to be used in the blank spaces. The quiz is placed at the end of each chapter. The quizzes can be done either as a test or as a group assignment.

Unit Crossword Puzzle

The *Unit Crossword Puzzle* in each chapter is based on the vocabulary used in that chapter. Students can go over the puzzle orally if pronunciation practice with letters is needed. The teacher can have students spell out their answers in addition to pronouncing the word itself. Students invariably enjoy doing crossword puzzles. They are a fun way to reinforce the vocabulary presented in the various exercises in each chapter, and require students to pay attention to correct spelling. At the same time, students need to connect the meaning of a word and think of the word itself. If the teacher prefers, students can do the crossword puzzle on their own or with a partner in their free time, or after they have completed an in-class assignment and are waiting for the rest of their classmates to finish.

Unit Discussion

This section contains questions which help students connect the related topics in the three chapters for that unit. The questions may be discussed in class or assigned as written homework.

Index of Key Words and Phrases

This section contains words and phrases from all the chapters for easy reference. It is located after the last chapter. *The Index of Key Words and Phrases* may be useful to students to help them locate words they need or wish to review.

ACKNOWLEDGMENTS

We are thankful to everyone at Heinle, especially Sherrise Roehr, Tom Jefferies, Laura Le Dréan, Susan Johnson, and Maryellen Killeen. As always, we are very appreciative of the ongoing encouragement from our family and friends.

L.C.S. and N.N.M.

Trends in Living

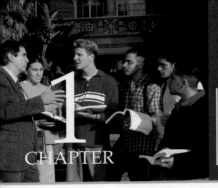

A Cultural Difference: Being on Time

CHAPTER 1

Prereading Preparation

1. What does **on time** mean?

_____

2. Is it always important to be on time? Look at the table on page 3. How important is it to be on time for each appointment? Put a check mark in the box to show your answer. Discuss your answers with the class.

3. Are you usually on time, or are you usually late? Why?

_____

4. Read the title of the article. What do you think this article is about?

_____

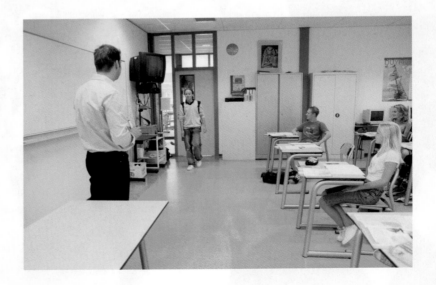

HOW IMPORTANT IS IT TO BE ON TIME?				
Type of Appointment	Scheduled Time	Very Important	Slightly Important	Not Important
dentist	9 A.M.			
university class	11 A.M.			
lunch with a friend at school	12 P.M.			
dinner with your spouse	7 P.M.			
a friend's party	9 P.M.			
job interview in a bank	2 P.M.			

Track 1

A Cultural Difference: Being on Time

1   In the United States, it is important to be on time, or punctual, for an
2 appointment, a class, a meeting, etc. However, this may not be true in all
3 countries. An American professor discovered this difference while teaching a
4 class in a Brazilian university. The two-hour class was scheduled to begin at
5 10 A.M. and end at 12 P.M. On the first day, when the professor arrived on time,
6 no one was in the classroom. Many students came after 10 A.M. Several arrived
7 after 10:30 A.M. Two students came after 11 A.M. Although all the students greeted
8 the professor as they arrived, few apologized for their lateness. Were these students
9 being rude? He decided to study the students' behavior.
10   The professor talked to American and Brazilian students about lateness in
11 both an informal and a formal situation: lunch with a friend and in a university
12 class, respectively. He gave them an example and asked them how they would
13 react. If they had a lunch appointment with a friend, the average American
14 student defined lateness as 19 minutes after the agreed time. On the other hand,
15 the average Brazilian student felt the friend was late after 33 minutes.

16 In an American university, students are expected to arrive at the appointed
17 hour. In contrast, in Brazil, neither the teacher nor the students always arrive at
18 the appointed hour. Classes not only begin at the scheduled time in the United
19 States, but they also end at the scheduled time. In the Brazilian class, only a few
20 students left the class at noon; many remained past 12:30 P.M. to discuss the class
21 and ask more questions. While arriving late may not be very important in Brazil,
22 neither is staying late.

23   The explanation for these differences is complicated. People from Brazilian
24 and North American cultures have different feelings about lateness. In Brazil,
25 the students believe that a person who usually arrives late is probably more
26 successful than a person who is always on time. In fact, Brazilians expect a
27 person with status or prestige to arrive late, while in the United States lateness
28 is usually considered to be disrespectful and unacceptable. Consequently, if a
29 Brazilian is late for an appointment with a North American, the American may
30 misinterpret the reason for the lateness and become angry.

31   As a result of his study, the professor learned that the Brazilian students
32 were not being disrespectful to him. Instead, they were simply behaving in the
33 appropriate way for a Brazilian student in Brazil. Eventually, the professor was
34 able to adapt his own behavior so that he could feel comfortable in the new
35 culture.

Fact-Finding Exercise

Read the passage again. Read the following statements. Check whether they are True or False. If a statement is false, rewrite the statement so that it is true. Then go back to the passage and find the line that supports your answer.

1 _____ True _____ False   On the first day of class, the professor arrived late, but the students were on time.

_____

2 _____ True _____ False   The professor decided to study the behavior of Brazilian and American students.

_____

3 _____ True _____ False   In an American university, it is important to be on time.

_____

4 _____ True _____ False   In a Brazilian class, the students leave immediately after the class is finished.

_____

5 _____ True _____ False   In an American university, many students probably leave immediately after the class is finished.

_____

6 _____ True _____ False   Most North Americans think a person who is late is disrespectful.

_____

7 _____ True _____ False   In Brazil, most successful people are expected to be on time.

_____

8 _____ True _____ False   As a result of the study, the professor changed the Brazilian students' behavior.

_____

Reading Analysis

Read each question carefully. Circle the letter or the number of the correct answer, or write your answer in the space provided.

1 What is the main idea of the passage?

   a. It is important to be on time for class in the United States.

   b. People learn the importance of time when they are children.

   c. The importance of being on time differs among cultures.

2 Why did the professor study the Brazilian students' behavior?

   a. The students seemed very rude to him.

   b. He wanted to understand why the students came late.

   c. He wanted to make the students come to class on time.

3 Read lines 1 and 2.

   a. What does **punctual** mean?

_____

   b. How do you know?

_____

4 In line 8, what does **few** refer to?

   a. The professor

   b. The students

   c. Greetings

5 Read lines 7–9.

   a. What does **as** mean?

     1. Because

     2. When

     3. If

   b. What is **rude behavior?**

     1. Impolite behavior

     2. Noisy behavior

     3. Studious behavior

6 **a.** Read lines 10–12. Which is an example of an informal situation?

_____

b. Which is an example of a formal situation?

_____

c. How do you know?

_____

d. What does this word mean?
  1. The same as
  2. In the same order
  3. Opposite

7 Read lines 13–15. How does **on the other hand** connect the American idea of lateness with the Brazilian idea of lateness?
  a. It shows a similarity.
  b. It gives more information.
  c. It shows a contrast.

8 Read lines 17 and 18: "Neither the teacher nor the students always arrive at the appointed hour." Who arrives at the appointed hour?
  a. No one
  b. The students only
  c. The teacher and the students

9 Read lines 18 and 19: "Classes not only begin at the scheduled time in the United States, but they also end at the scheduled time." What does **not only . . . but . . . also** mean?
  a. And
  b. But
  c. So

10 In line 26, what does **in fact** indicate?
  a. A contrast between two ideas
  b. Something that is true
  c. Emphasis of the previous idea

11 Read lines 31–33. What does **instead** show?
  a. A similarity
  b. A substitution
  c. An opposite

Information Organization

Read the passage again. Underline what you think are the main ideas. Then scan the reading and complete the following flowchart about the reading. Use the sentences that you have underlined to help you. You will use this flowchart later to answer questions about the reading.

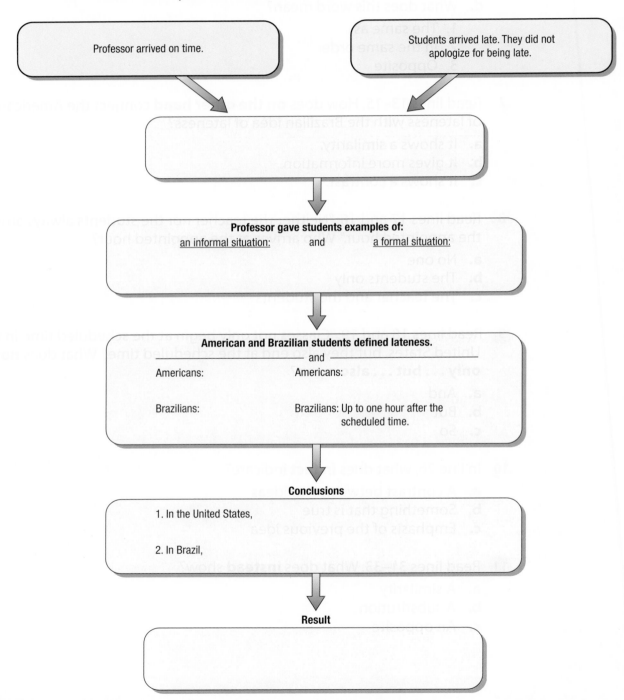

Professor arrived on time.

Students arrived late. They did not apologize for being late.

Professor gave students examples of:
an informal situation: _____ and _____ a formal situation:

American and Brazilian students defined lateness.
_____ and _____
Americans: _____   Americans:

Brazilians: Brazilians: Up to one hour after the scheduled time.

Conclusions

1. In the United States,

2. In Brazil,

Result

Information Recall and Summary

Read each question carefully. Use your flowchart to answer the questions. Do not refer back to the passage. When you are finished, write a brief summary of the reading.

1. What did the professor decide to study?

   _____

2. Describe the professor's experiment.

   _____

   _____

3. Did American students and Brazilian students have the same ideas about lateness in class? Do classes always begin and end at the appointed hour in both cultures?

   _____

   _____

4. What were the American students' and the Brazilian students' ideas about being late for a lunch appointment?

   _____

   _____

5. In general, what did the Brazilian students think about people who are late?

   _____

6. In general, what did the American students think about people who are late?

   _____

7. What was the result of the professor's study?

   _____

Summary

Work in pairs or alone. Write a brief summary of the reading, and put it on the board. Compare your summary with your classmates'. Which one best describes the main idea of the reading?

_____

_____

_____

_____

E

Dictionary Skills

Read the following sentences. Use the context to help you understand the boldface words. Read the dictionary entry for that word and circle the appropriate definition. Then choose the sentence with the correct answer.

1   **react** *v.* [I] **1** to speak or move when s.t. happens: *When he heard the good news, he reacted with a smile.* **2** to act in a different way because of s.o. or s.t.: *The teacher reacted to the student's bad grades by giving him more homework.* **3** (in chemistry) to change because of contact with another chemical: *Oxygen and iron react together to form rust.*

The professor gave American and Brazilian students an example and asked them how they would **react**.

   a. The professor gave American and Brazilian students an example and asked them how they would respond in this situation.

   b. The professor gave American and Brazilian students an example and asked them how they would act in a different way in this situation.

   c. The professor gave American and Brazilian students an example and asked them how they would change because of contact with a chemical in this situation.

> **2**   **discover** *v.* **1** [I; T] to learn, find out: *When she got to her door, she discovered she had lost her key.* **2** [T] to find, see, or learn of (s.t. no one knew before): *Galileo discovered the planet Jupiter.* **3** [T] to invent: *Scientists in England discovered penicillin.*

An American professor **discovered** this difference while teaching a class in a Brazilian university.

   a. An American professor invented this difference while teaching a class in a Brazilian university.

   b. An American professor learned something that no one knew before about this difference while teaching a class in a Brazilian university.

   c. An American professor found out this difference while teaching a class in a Brazilian university.

F   Word Forms

PART 1

In English, verbs change to nouns in several ways. Some verbs become nouns by adding the suffix *-ation*—for example, *combine (v.)* becomes *combination (n.)*. Complete each sentence with the correct form of the words on the left. **Use the correct tense of the verb in either the affirmative or the negative form. Use the singular or plural form of the noun.**

adapt *(v.)*

adaptation *(n.)*

1 Next year a big film company _____ a story from a book to make a movie. The _____ of a book to a movie takes a lot of work and time.

interpret (v.)

interpretation (n.)

2 Chris is studying at the university for a degree in _____. When he graduates, he _____ for an embassy.

expect (v.)

expectation (n.)

3 Most people have high _____ when they visit another country. They _____ to have a bad time. They want to enjoy themselves.

observe (v.)

observation (n.)

4 Suzie is in the park now. She _____ the behavior of pigeons. She records all her _____ in a special notebook.

explain (v.)

explanation (n.)

5 We needed an _____ of the difference between adjectives and adverbs. The teacher _____ the difference to us, and we understood.

PART 2

In English, verbs change to nouns in several ways. Some verbs become nouns by adding the suffix -ing—for example, *feel (v.)* becomes *feeling (n.)*. Complete each sentence with the correct form of the words on the left. **Use the correct tense of the verb in either the affirmative or the negative form. Use the singular or plural form of the noun.**

spell (v.)

spelling (n.)

1 Allen _____ several words incorrectly on his composition yesterday. He has to check the _____ of a difficult word before he uses it.

understand (v.)

understanding (n.)

2 Andrew _____ anything in his first math class yesterday. However, his _____ will improve during the semester.

end (v.)

ending (n.)

3 Please don't tell me the _____ of this mystery story. I want to guess how the story _____ by myself.

greet (v.)	4	"Hi," "Hello," and "How are you" are common
greeting (n.)		_____ in the United States. Most people also
		_____ each other with a smile.
meet (v.)	5	Our department has ten monthly _____ every year.
meeting (n.)		We _____ during May or December.

Word Partnership	Use *meeting* with:
n.	meeting **agenda, board** meeting, **business** meeting
v.	**attend** a meeting, **call** a meeting, **go to** a meeting, **have** a meeting, **hold** a meeting, **plan** a meeting, **schedule** a meeting

G

Vocabulary in Context

adapt (v.)	greets (v.)	rude (adj.)
apologized (v.)	in fact	unacceptable (adj.)
appropriate (adj.)	prestige (n.)	
behavior (n.)	punctual (adj.)	

Read the following sentences. Complete each blank space with the correct word or phrase from the list above. Use each word or phrase only once.

1 A suit and tie are _____ clothes for a business meeting.

2 Wearing shorts in a church is _____.

3 In most countries, doctors have considerable _____. People respect them highly.

4 Greg always _____ people by smiling and saying hello.

5 It was very _____ of Martin to ask Mrs. Barnes her age.

6 Being _____ for a job interview is important in order to make a good impression.

7 When you walk into a dark room from the bright sunlight, your eyes need a few moments to _____ to the change in light.

8 It is very cold in Antarctica. _____, it is the coldest place on Earth.

9 Martha dropped chocolate ice cream on my white rug. She _____, but I told her not to worry about it, and we cleaned it up.

10 I don't understand Mark's _____. He gets angry for no reason and refuses to talk to anyone.

H

Critical Thinking Strategies

Read the following questions and think about the answers. Write your answer below each question. Then compare your answers with those of your classmates.

1 How do you think the professor adapted his behavior in Brazil after his study?

_____

_____

2 Why do you think the professor changed his behavior? Why didn't he try to change the Brazilian students' behavior?

_____

_____

Topics for Discussion and Writing

I

1. Describe how people in your culture feel about someone who is late. For example, do you think that person is inconsiderate and irresponsible, or do you think that person is prestigious and successful? Please explain your answer, and also give some examples.

2. When you travel to a new place, what kinds of adaptations or changes (for example, food, currency, etc.) do you have to make? Explain your answer.

3. **Write in your journal.** Do you think it is important to adapt your behavior to a new culture? In what ways would you be willing to make changes? Please explain.

Follow-Up Activity

J

There are many differences in customs among cultures. In the table below, list some cultural differences between this country and your country, or between your country and another country you have visited. Compare your list with your classmates' lists.

Cultural Difference	_____ (Your Country)	_____ (Other Country)
1. clothes: school work		
2.		
3.		
4.		
5.		

Cloze Quiz

Read the passage below. Fill in the blanks with one word from the list. Use each word only once.

adapt	ended	instead	only
appointment	fact	late	punctual
behavior	formal	misinterpret	rude
contrast	greeted	neither	status
difference	hand	nor	unacceptable

In the United States, it is important to be on time, or _____ (1), for an appointment, a class, a meeting, etc. However, this may not be true in all countries. An American professor discovered this _____ (2) while teaching a class in a Brazilian university. The two-hour class began at 10 A.M. and _____ (3) at 12 P.M. On the first day, when the professor arrived on time, no one was in the classroom. Many students came after 10 A.M. Several arrived after 10:30 A.M. Two students came after 11 A.M. Although all the students _____ (4) the professor as they arrived, few apologized for their lateness. Were these students being _____ (5)? He decided to study the students' _____ (6).

The professor talked to American and Brazilian students about lateness in both an informal and a _____ (7) situation: lunch with a friend and in a university class. He gave them an example and asked them how they would react. If they had a lunch _____ (8) with a friend, the average American student defined lateness as 19 minutes after the agreed time. On the other _____ (9), the average Brazilian student felt the friend was late after 33 minutes.

In an American university, students are expected to arrive at the appointed hour. In _____ (10), in Brazil, neither the teacher _____ (11) the students always arrive at the appointed hour. Classes not _____ (12) begin at the scheduled time in the United States, but they also end at the scheduled time. In the Brazilian class, only a few students left the class at noon; many remained past 12:30 P.M. to discuss the class and ask more questions. While arriving late may not be very important in Brazil, _____ (13) is staying late.

The explanation for these differences is complicated. People from Brazilian and North American cultures have different feelings about lateness. In Brazil, the students believe that a person who usually arrives _____ (14) is probably more successful than a person who is always on time. In _____ (15), Brazilians expect a person with _____ (16) or prestige to arrive late, while in the United States lateness is usually disrespectful and _____ (17). Consequently, if a Brazilian is late for an appointment with a North American, the American may _____ (18) the reason for the lateness and become angry.

As a result of his study, the professor learned that the Brazilian students were not being disrespectful to him. _____ (19), they were simply behaving in the appropriate way for a Brazilian student in Brazil. Eventually, the professor was able to _____ (20) his own behavior so that he could feel comfortable in the new culture.

2 CHAPTER

Changing Lifestyles and New Eating Habits

Prereading Preparation

1 What are **lifestyles?** Give examples of two very different lifestyles. Describe how they are different.

_____

_____

2 Think about your life today. Is your life different today from the way it was three or four years ago? Write about some differences in your life now. List them in the chart below, and tell a classmate about them.

My Life Today	My Life 3 or 4 Years Ago

3 How do you think American lifestyles are changing? Read the title of this article. What do you think this article is about? What examples do you think the author will give?

_____

_____

Track 2

Changing Lifestyles and New Eating Habits

1   Americans today have different eating habits than they had in the past. There
2 is a wide selection of food available. They have a broader knowledge of nutrition,
3 so they buy more fresh fruit and vegetables than ever before. At the same time,
4 Americans purchase increasing quantities of sweets, snacks, and sodas.
5   Statistics show that the way people live determines the way they eat.
6 American lifestyles have changed. They now include growing numbers of
7 people who live alone, single parents and children, and double-income families.
8 These changing lifestyles are responsible for the increasing number of people
9 who must rush meals or sometimes skip them altogether. Many Americans have
10 less time than ever before to spend preparing food. Partly as a consequence of
11 this limited time, more than 90% of all American homes now have microwave
12 ovens. Moreover, Americans eat out nearly four times a week on the average.
13   It is easy to study the amounts and kinds of food that people consume. The
14 United States Department of Agriculture (USDA) and the food industry—
15 growers, processors, marketers, and restaurateurs—compile sales statistics
16 and keep accurate records. This information not only tells us what people are
17 eating, but also tells us about the changes in attitudes and tastes. Red meat,
18 which used to be the most popular choice for dinner, is no longer an American
19 favorite. Instead, chicken, turkey, and fish have become more popular. Sales of
20 these foods have greatly increased in recent years. This is probably a result of the
21 awareness of the dangers of eating food that contains high levels of cholesterol,
22 or animal fat. Doctors believe that cholesterol is a threat to human health.
23   According to a recent survey, Americans also change their eating patterns to
24 meet the needs of different situations. They have certain ideas about which foods
25 will increase their athletic ability, help them lose weight, make them alert for
26 business meetings, or put them in the mood for romance. For example, Americans

27 choose pasta, fruit, and vegetables, which supply them with carbohydrates, to give
28 them strength for physical activity, such as sports. Adults choose foods rich in fiber,
29 such as bread and cereal, for breakfast, and salads for lunch to prepare them for
30 business appointments. For romantic dinners, however, Americans choose shrimp
31 and lobster. While many of these ideas are based on nutritional facts, some are not.
32   Americans' awareness of nutrition, along with their changing tastes and
33 needs, leads them to consume a wide variety of foods—foods for health, for fun,
34 and simply for good taste.

Fact-Finding Exercise

Read the passage again. Read the following statements. Check whether they are True or False. If a statement is false, rewrite the statement so that it is true. Then go back to the passage and find the line that supports your answer.

1 _____ True _____ False   Americans eat the same way they did in the past.

_____

2 _____ True _____ False   Americans do not eat many sweets anymore.

_____

3 _____ True _____ False   Most Americans do not have a lot of time to prepare food.

_____

4 _____ True _____ False Red meat is the most popular American choice for dinner.

_____

5 _____ True _____ False Americans eat out about four times a week.

_____

6 _____ True _____ False The USDA keeps information about the food Americans buy.

_____

7 _____ True _____ False It is healthy to eat food with high cholesterol levels.

_____

8 _____ True _____ False Americans choose foods rich in fiber for romantic dinners.

_____

B Reading Analysis

Read each question carefully. Circle the letter or the number of the correct answer, or write your answer in the space provided.

1 What is the main idea of the passage?
   a. American eating habits have changed because of changing lifestyles.
   b. Americans have a greater awareness of nutrition than they did years ago.
   c. Americans have less time than ever before to prepare meals.

2 In lines 3–4, what are **quantities?**
   a. Kinds
   b. Amounts
   c. Types

3 Read lines 5–7.
   a. What are **lifestyles?**
      1. The way people live
      2. The way people eat
      3. The way people dress

b. What is a **double-income family?**

    1. A family that makes twice as much money as another family

    2. A family in which one adult has two jobs

    3. A family in which two adults work full-time

4 Read line 12. What does **on the average** mean?

    a. Exactly

    b. Approximately

    c. Sometimes

5 In lines 13–16, what are examples of jobs in the food industry?

_____

6 Read lines 17–19. What is **red meat?**

    a. Chicken

    b. Fish

    c. Beef

7 Read lines 20–22.

    a. What is **cholesterol?**

_____

    b. How do you know?

_____

8 In lines 30 and 31, what does **however** indicate?

    a. An explanation

    b. A similarity

    c. A contrast

9 Read line 30.

    a. What does **while** mean?

        1. During

        2. Although

        3. Also

    b. What does **some** refer to?

        1. Ideas

        2. Facts

        3. Americans

10 In line 32, what does **along with** mean?

    a. Except for

    b. Together with

    c. Instead of

Information Organization

Read the passage again. Underline what you think are the main ideas. Then scan the reading and complete the following flowchart about the reading. Use the sentences that you have underlined to help you. You will use this flowchart later to answer questions about the reading.

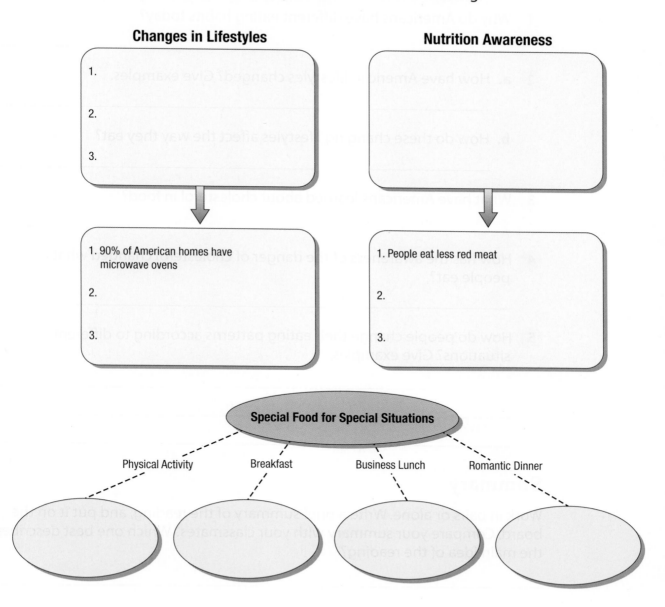

Changes in Lifestyles

1.
2.
3.

Nutrition Awareness

1. 90% of American homes have microwave ovens
2.
3.

1. People eat less red meat
2.
3.

Special Food for Special Situations

Physical Activity   Breakfast   Business Lunch   Romantic Dinner

Information Recall and Summary

Read each question carefully. Use your flowchart to answer the questions. Do not refer back to the passage. When you are finished, write a brief summary of the reading.

1 Why do Americans have different eating habits today?

_____

2 a. How have American lifestyles changed? Give examples.

   _____

   b. How do these changing lifestyles affect the way they eat?

   _____

3 What have Americans learned about cholesterol in food?

_____

4 How has the awareness of the danger of cholesterol changed what people eat?

_____

5 How do people change their eating patterns according to different situations? Give examples.

_____

_____

_____

Summary

Work in pairs or alone. Write a brief summary of the reading, and put it on the board. Compare your summary with your classmates'. Which one best describes the main idea of the reading?

_____

_____

_____

Dictionary Skills

Read the following sentences. Use the context to help you understand the boldface words. Read the dictionary entry for that word and circle the appropriate definition. Then choose the sentence with the correct answer.

1 **rush** *v. -es* **1** [I; T] to move about doing things quickly, hurry: *She rushed to get ready for an evening at the theater.* **2** [I; T] to move quickly: *When she fell, a friend rushed to help her get up.* **3** *phrasal v. insep.* [T] **to rush in/into s.t.: a.** to enter a place quickly, run into: *Firefighters rushed into the building to save people from the fire.* **b.** to make a decision too quickly, without thinking: *I don't think that you should rush into getting married so young.* **4** *phrasal v.* [I] **to rush over:** to go someplace quickly: *When I saw that my friend was hurt, I rushed over to help her.*

These changing lifestyles are responsible for the increasing number of people who must **rush** meals.

  a. These changing lifestyles are responsible for the increasing number of people who must make decisions very quickly about eating meals.
  b. These changing lifestyles are responsible for the increasing number of people who must move about quickly when they eat meals.
  c. These changing lifestyles are responsible for the increasing number of people who must eat meals very quickly.

2 **skip** *v.* **skipped, skipping, skips** **1** [I] to run in a hopping way: *The little girl skipped happily to her friend's house.* **2** [T] to use a jump rope: *to skip rope* **3** [I; T] not to do s.t. that one usu. does, to miss: *to skip a meal | | to skip school for a day* **4** [I; T] to pass over: *I read Chapters 2 and 4, but skipped Chapter 3.*

These changing lifestyles are responsible for the increasing number of people who must rush meals or sometimes **skip** them entirely.

  a. These changing lifestyles are responsible for the increasing number of people who must rush meals or sometimes not eat them at all.
  b. These changing lifestyles are responsible for the increasing number of people who must rush meals or sometimes run in a hopping way to them.
  c. These changing lifestyles are responsible for the increasing number of people who must rush meals or sometimes pass over them entirely.

> **3** | **alert** *adj.* **1** aware, *(syn.)* attentive: *The guard stayed alert to watch for anything unusual.* **2** bright, intelligent: *Their son is an alert little boy.*

Americans have certain ideas about which foods will make them **alert** for business meetings.

a. Americans have certain ideas about which foods will make them intelligent for business meetings.

b. Americans have certain ideas about which foods will make them attentive for business meetings.

F Word Forms

PART 1

In English, verbs change to nouns in several ways. Some verbs become nouns that represent people by adding the suffix -er—for example, *teach (v.)* becomes *teacher (n.).* Complete each sentence with the correct form of the words on the left. **Use the correct tense of the verb in either the affirmative or the negative form. Use the singular or plural form of the noun.**

grow *(v.)*

grower *(n.)*

1 Thomas _____ flowers in his garden. He only plants vegetables. He is an expert, so other _____ in his neighborhood often ask him for advice.

market *(v.)*

marketer *(n.)*

2 The various _____ of fruit must ship their produce in refrigerated trucks. They _____ a new type of apple next season.

consume *(v.)*

consumer *(n.)*

3 Enthusiastic _____ of fruit are very demanding. They want only the freshest fruit. They _____ tons of fruit every year.

employ *(v.)*
employer *(n.)*

4 When she began her own company, Ms. Harris _____ anyone who had very little experience. Like other _____, she wanted experienced people who didn't need much training.

work *(v.)*
worker *(n.)*

5 Mark is a very dependable _____. He always _____ hard and does his job well.

PART 2

In English, adjectives can change to verbs. Some adjectives become verbs by adding the suffix -en—for example, *light (adj.)* becomes *lighten (v.)*. Complete each sentence with the correct form of the words on the left. **Use the correct tense of the verb in either the affirmative or the negative form.**

long *(adj.)*
lengthen *(v.)*

1 The American government _____ some weekends because midweek holidays are inconvenient. Now some holidays are celebrated on Monday, so everyone has a _____ weekend.

wide *(adj.)*
widen *(v.)*

2 The government _____ the old highway, although it is too narrow. Instead, the government is planning a new highway, which will be very _____.

sweet *(adj.)*
sweeten *(v.)*

3 Joseph loves to drink very _____ coffee. He _____ his coffee by adding four teaspoons of sugar to his cup.

short (adj.)

shorten (v.)

(4) The factory workers want a _____ work week, so they had a demonstration at the factory. The company _____ their work week to only four days a week next month.

broad (adj.)

broaden (v.)

(5) Betty went to college to study French, but she felt that her major was not _____ enough. Next semester she _____ her major to romance languages, and study Spanish and Portuguese as well as French.

Word Partnership	Use *broad* with:
n.	broad **expanse**, broad **shoulders**, broad **smile**, broad **range**, broad **spectrum**, broad **definition**, broad **strokes**, broad **view**

G Vocabulary in Context

alert *(adj.)*	**habit** *(n.)*	**survey** *(n.)*
awareness *(n.)*	**nutritional** *(adj.)*	**variety** *(n.)*
compile *(v.)*	**rush** *(v.)*	
favorite *(adj.)*	**skip** *(v.)*	

Read the following sentences. Complete each blank space with the correct word from the list above. Use each word only once.

1. Children like a _____ of food in their diet. For example, at breakfast they like to choose among cereal, pancakes, doughnuts, or eggs and toast.

2. If you do not understand one part of the test, you can _____ to the next part and go back to the difficult part later.

3. Joan's train was scheduled to leave at 6 P.M. It was 5:50, so she had to _____ in order not to miss her train.

4. Dean and Jenny are going to _____ a list of all the places they want to visit on their next trip across the country.

5. I like all kinds of cake, cookies, and ice cream, but my _____ dessert is chocolate ice cream. I like it best of all!

6. The college cafeteria manager is going to do a _____ of the students to help her decide which foods students prefer.

7. Small children have very little _____ of the dangers of running into the street.

8. Fruit and vegetables are an important part of a _____ diet.

9. Many students drink large quantities of coffee to keep them _____ while they are studying for an important exam.

10. Ann has a _____ of doing her homework as soon as she gets home from school.

Critical Thinking Strategies

Read the following questions and think about the answers. Write your answer below each question. Then compare your answers with those of your classmates.

1   Many Americans have less time than ever before to spend preparing food. What do you think are some reasons for this?

_____

_____

2   Americans choose shrimp and lobster for romantic dinners. Why do you think they do this?

_____

_____

Topics for Discussion and Writing

1   Are lifestyles also changing in your country? Why? Describe how they are changing. Are they similar to the lifestyles in the United States today?

2   In your country, do people eat differently today than they did in the past? Give reasons and examples in your explanation.

3   In your country, what do you eat in various situations (for example, to increase athletic ability, to lose weight, to be alert for business, for romance)? Why?

4   Look at the chart on the following page. In 1790, most U.S. households had 7 or more persons. What do you think are some reasons for this large number? Talk about your ideas with your classmates, and then write a paragraph explaining your answer.

5   **Write in your journal.** Describe your present lifestyle. What do you like about it? What do you dislike about it?

Follow-Up Activities

U.S. Households by Size, 1790–2006

The following table shows the number of U.S. households, the percent distribution of the number of people in those households, and the average population per household for select years from 1790 to 2006.

Year	Number of households (in thousands)	PERCENT DISTRIBUTION OF NUMBER OF HOUSEHOLDS						
		1 person	2 persons	3 persons	4 persons	5 persons	6 persons	7 or more persons
1790	558	3.7%	7.8%	11.7%	13.8%	13.9%	13.2%	35.8%
1890	12,690	3.6	13.2	16.7	16.8	15.1	11.6	23.0
1900	15,964	5.1	15.0	17.6	16.9	14.2	10.9	20.4
1950	43,468	10.9	28.8	22.6	17.8	10.0	5.1	4.9
1960	52,610	13.1	27.8	18.9	17.6	11.5	5.7	5.4
1970	62,874	17.0	28.8	17.3	15.8	10.4	5.6	5.1
1980	80,776	22.7	31.3	17.5	15.7	7.5	3.1	2.2
1990	93,347	24.6	32.2	17.2	15.5	6.7	2.3	1.4
1995	98,990	25.0	32.1	17.0	15.5	6.7	2.3	1.4
2000	104,705	25.5	33.1	16.4	14.6	6.7	2.3	1.4
2003	111,278	26.4	33.3	16.1	14.3	6.3	2.3	1.2
2006	114,400	27.0	33.0	17.0	14.0	6.0	2.0	1.0

1 Refer to the chart above. Read the following sentences and fill in the blank spaces with the correct year.

    a. The smallest number of 1-person households was in _____.

    b. Most households had 7 or more persons in _____.

    c. Only 1% of all households had 7 or more persons in _____.

    d. The largest number of 2-person households was in _____.

    e. The largest number of 4-person households was in _____.

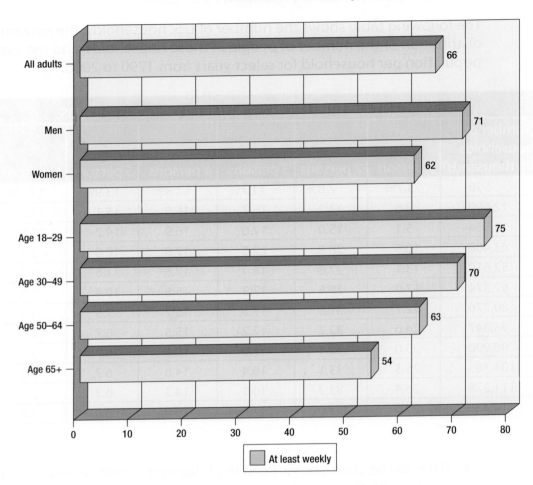

How Often Do You Eat Out?
Percent who say they eat a meal at a
restaurant at least weekly

All adults — 66
Men — 71
Women — 62
Age 18–29 — 75
Age 30–49 — 70
Age 50–64 — 63
Age 65+ — 54

0 10 20 30 40 50 60 70 80

At least weekly

2 Refer to the chart above. Answer the following questions.

  a. Who eats out most often? _____
  What do you think are some reasons for this?

  _____

  b. Who eats out the least? _____
  What do you think are some reasons for this?

  _____

  c. Who eats out more often: men or women? _____
  What do you think are some reasons for this?

  _____

3 Many different factors can affect the way we eat. For example, if you are a very busy person, you may not have a lot of time for meals. As a result, you may not cook very much or you may eat out often. On the other hand, you may have a lot of free time. How would this affect your eating habits? Think about some different factors, list them below, and write about how they affect eating habits.

Factor	Effect on Eating Habits
1. time	
2. money	
3.	
4.	
5.	

Cloze Quiz

Read the passage below. Fill in the blanks with one word from the list. Use each word only once.

alert	consequence	however	recent
along	consume	lifestyles	skip
average	example	nearly	survey
awareness	favorite	nutrition	threat
compile	habits	quantities	variety

Americans today have different eating _____ than in the past.
(1)
There is a wide selection of food available. They have a broader knowledge
of _____, so they buy more fresh fruit and vegetables than ever before.
(2)
At the same time, Americans purchase increasing _____ of sweets,
(3)
snacks, and sodas.

Statistics show that the way people live determines the way they eat.
American _____ have changed. They now include growing numbers
(4)
of people who live alone, single parents and children, and double-income
families. These changing lifestyles are responsible for the increasing number
of people who must rush meals or sometimes _____ them altogether.
(5)
Many Americans have less time than ever before to spend preparing
food. Partly as a _____ of this limited time, more than 90% of all
(6)
American homes now have microwave ovens. Moreover, Americans eat out
_____ four times a week on the _____.
(7)   (8)

It is easy to study the amounts and kinds of food that people _____.
(9)
The United States Department of Agriculture (USDA) and the food
industry—growers, processors, marketers, and restaurateurs— _____
(10)

sales statistics and keep accurate records. This information not only tells us what people are eating, but also tells us about the changes in attitudes and tastes. Red meat, which used to be the most popular choice for dinner, is no longer an American _____. Instead, chicken, turkey, and fish
(11)
have become more popular. Sales of these foods have greatly increased in _____ years. This is probably a result of the _____ of the
(12)   (13)
dangers of eating food that contains high levels of cholesterol, or animal fat. Doctors believe that cholesterol is a _____ to human health.
(14)

   According to a recent _____, Americans also change their eating
(15)
patterns to meet the needs of different situations. They have certain ideas about which foods will increase their athletic ability, help them lose weight, make them _____ for business meetings, or put them in the mood for
(16)
romance. For _____, Americans choose pasta, fruit, and vegetables,
(17)
which supply them with carbohydrates, to give them strength for physical activity, such as sports. Adults choose foods rich in fiber, such as bread and cereal, for breakfast, and salads for lunch to prepare them for business appointments. For romantic dinners, _____, Americans choose shrimp
(18)
and lobster. While many of these ideas are based on nutritional facts, some are not. Americans' awareness of nutrition, _____ with their changing
(19)
tastes and needs, leads them to consume a wide _____ of foods—
(20)
foods for health, for fun, and simply for good taste.

3 CHAPTER

Technology Competes for Family Time

Prereading Preparation

1 Look at the photo. Describe it. Who are these people? What are they doing?

2 Answer the questions in the chart below. Then compare your answers with your classmates' answers.

Each week, how much time do you spend	Number of Hours
1. watching TV?	
2. surfing the Internet?	
3. talking on your cell phone?	
4. playing computer games?	
Total Number of Hours	
5. speaking with your family?	
Difference between 1–4 and 5	

3 Read the title of this chapter, and review your chart.
   a. Do you spend more time with technology, or more time with your family?
   b. Is it important to spend time with your family? Why or why not?

Technology Competes for Family Time

1   When the Johnson family bought their first computer several years ago,
2   Mr. and Mrs. Johnson were thrilled that their children had access to so much
3   information through the Internet. Now, though, they're not as excited anymore.
4   "Our family spends more time surfing the Internet than communicating with
5   each other," complains Mr. Johnson. The Johnson family is not alone in this
6   situation. According to research by the Annenberg Center for the Digital Future at
7   the University of Southern California, in 2006, 11% of Americans said they were
8   spending less time with their families. Last year, the number almost tripled to 28%.

9   It seems that as Internet use becomes more popular, the amount of family
10 time decreases. Many parents are concerned about this reduction in the time
11 their families spend together, and Michael Gilbert agrees. He is a researcher at
12 the Annenberg Center. "Most people think of the Internet and our digital future
13 as boundless—unlimited—, and I do too," Gilbert said. However, he added, "It
14 can't be a good thing that families are spending less face-to-face time together."

15 As technology becomes more advanced, it often changes the ways that families
16 interact. This is not a new concern. When televisions first became popular in the 1950s,
17 parents worried that their children were watching too much TV and spending too
18 little time talking with their parents. However, there is a significant difference between
19 these two activities. Watching TV can be done as a family, while surfing the Internet
20 is often a solitary activity. Furthermore, the Internet isn't the only modern technology
21 pushing families apart. Many children today have cell phones. Although they help
22 parents to keep track of their children, cell phones also give children more privacy.
23 Sometimes they have too much privacy. "When I was a teenager," Mrs. Johnson says,
24 "my friends telephoned me at home. My parents always knew who was calling me."

25 From 2000 to 2005, people spent about 26 hours each month with their families. A
26 few years later, that number dropped to about 18 hours, according to the Annenberg
27 Study. In addition to reduced face-to-face time among all family members, women
28 say that they feel ignored by a family Internet user. In fact, almost half say they are
29 sometimes or often ignored, while fewer than forty percent of men feel this way.

30 Gilbert said, "People report spending less time with family members as social
31 networks like Facebook, Twitter, and MySpace are booming." However, not all
32 young people enjoy the new technology that allows them to be in contact with
33 their friends around the clock. Steven Cho, a college student, is one of them.
34 Every summer he works at a camp in upstate New York. The camp has very little

35 Internet access. "It's nice to get away from the Internet for a few weeks every
36 summer," says Steven. "I can relax and do other things like play music, read, or be
37 with my friends." Although he spends a lot of time on the Internet during the
38 school year, he is happy to have a break from it. "It gets very tiring sometimes,"
39 he adds. The Internet is here to stay, and so are cell phones. How will families
40 change in the future as technology competes with their time together?

Fact-Finding Exercise

Read the passage again. Read the following statements. Check whether they
are True or False. If a statement is false, rewrite the statement so that it is true.
Then go back to the passage and find the line that supports your answer.

1 _____ True _____ False   The Johnson family spends most of their time
                                communicating with each other.

_____

2 _____ True _____ False   In 2006, Americans spent less time with their families than they do today.

_____

3 _____ True _____ False   Families spend less time together as computers become more popular.

_____

4 _____ True _____ False   Surfing the Internet is usually done as a family.

_____

5 _____ True _____ False   More women feel ignored by family Internet users than men do.

_____

6 _____ True _____ False   Michael Gilbert thinks families should spend more time together.

_____

7 _____ True _____ False   Young people can stay connected to their friends all day because of technology.

_____

8 _____ True _____ False   Steven Cho has very little Internet access at college.

_____

B Reading Analysis

Read each question carefully. Circle the letter or the number of the correct answer, or write your answer in the space provided.

1   What is the main idea of the passage?
   a. Family time decreases as technology becomes more popular.
   b. Family time increases as technology becomes more popular.
   c. Children have more privacy because of cell phones.

2 Read lines 1–3. What word is a synonym for **thrilled?**

_____

3 **a.** Read line 3. **They're not as excited anymore** because
1. their children don't enjoy the Internet
2. their children spend too much time on the Internet
3. their children like to communicate with each other

    b. Who are **they?**
1. Mr. and Mrs. Johnson
2. The children
3. The family

4 In lines 5–8, **the Johnson family is not alone in this situation** means
    a. many other families have the same problem
    b. the Johnson family has a lot of friends
    c. Mr. and Mrs. Johnson like to be alone with their family

5 Read lines 9–11.
    a. **Reduction** means
1. become more
2. stay the same
3. become less

    b. Who is Michael Gilbert?
1. A friend of the Johnson family
2. An Internet user
3. A technology researcher

6 In lines 12 and 13, what word is a synonym for **boundless?**

_____

7 Read lines 18–20. What is the **significant difference** between television and the Internet?
    a. Families cannot use the Internet together, but they can watch TV together.
    b. Families cannot watch TV together, but they can use the Internet together.
    c. Families can watch TV and use the Internet together.

8 In line 20, a **solitary activity** is

    a. something that people do together
    b. something you do with your family
    c. something a person does alone

9 Read lines 37 and 38. **He is happy to have a break from it.**

    a. Who is **he?**

        1. Steven Cho
        2. Mr. Johnson
        3. Michael Gilbert

    b. What is **it?**

        1. The TV
        2. The Internet
        3. His college

    c. **Have a break from** means

        1. get away from
        2. get information from
        3. get tired from

10 Read line 39. **The Internet is here to stay, and so are cell phones** means

    a. the Internet and cell phones stay in our homes
    b. some day people will not use cell phones and computers any more
    c. people will always have cell phones and computers

Information Organization

Read the passage again. Underline what you think are the main ideas. Then scan the reading and complete the following flowchart, using the sentences that you have underlined to help you. You will use this flowchart later to answer questions about the reading.

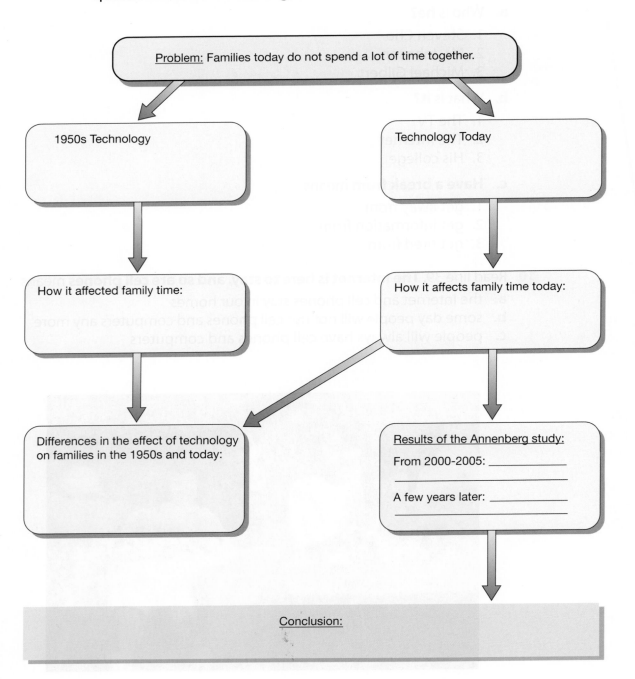

Problem: Families today do not spend a lot of time together.

1950s Technology

Technology Today

How it affected family time:

How it affects family time today:

Differences in the effect of technology on families in the 1950s and today:

Results of the Annenberg study:

From 2000-2005: _____
_____

A few years later: _____
_____

Conclusion:

D Information Recall and Summary

Read each question carefully. Use your flowchart to answer the questions. Do not refer back to the passage. When you are finished, write a brief summary of the reading.

1 **a.** What are some examples of 1950s technology?

_____

b. What are some examples of technology today?

_____

2 **a.** How did technology affect family time in the 1950s?

_____

b. How does technology affect family time today?

_____

3 What is the biggest difference between 1950s technology and technology today?

_____

4 What were the results of the Annenberg Study?

_____

5 What conclusion can we draw as a result of the Annenberg Study?

_____

Summary

Work in pairs or alone. Write a brief summary of the reading, and put it on the board. Compare your summary with your classmates'. Which one best describes the main idea of the reading?

_____

_____

E Dictionary Skills

Read the following sentences. Use the context to help you understand the boldface words. Read the dictionary entry for that word and circle the appropriate definition. Then choose the sentence with the correct answer.

1 | **surf** *v.* **1** [I] to ride the ocean's waves as they break in approaching the shore, esp. while standing on a narrow board (surfboard): *She went to California to surf.* **2** (in computers) **to surf the Net/the Web:** to search from place to place on the Internet for interesting information: *I surfed the Net for five hours yesterday.*

"Our family spends more time **surfing** the Internet than communicating with each other," complains Mr. Johnson.

a. "Our family spends more time riding waves on the Internet than communicating with each other," complains Mr. Johnson.

b. "Our family spends more time searching from place to place on the Internet than communicating with each other," complains Mr. Johnson.

2 | **access** *n.*[U] **1** entrance, permission to use: *I got access to the library by showing my identity card.* **2** a way or means of reaching or entering a place: *The only access to the island is by boat or plane.*

Mr. and Mrs. Johnson were thrilled that their children had **access** to so much information through the Internet.

a. Mr. and Mrs. Johnson were thrilled that their children had a way to get to so much information through the Internet.

b. Mr. and Mrs. Johnson were thrilled that their children had permission to use so much information through the Internet.

3 | **solitary** *adj.* **1** lone, single: *A solitary house stood in an open field.* **2** alone: *My aunt lives alone and likes her solitary life.*

Watching TV can be done as a family, while surfing the Internet is often a **solitary** activity.

a. Watching TV can be done as a family, while surfing the Internet is often a single activity that people do without doing anything else.

b. Watching TV can be done as a family, while surfing the Internet is often an activity that people do alone, with no one else.

Word Forms

In English, the verb and noun forms of some words are the same—for example, *research (n.)* and *research (v.)*. Complete each sentence with the correct form of the words on the left. **Use the correct tense of the verb in either the affirmative or the negative form. Use the singular or plural form of the noun. In addition, indicate whether you are using the noun (n.) or verb (v.) form.**

access

1 In most colleges, students _____ the Internet
(v., n.)

in classrooms, the library, or the cafeteria. This easy

_____ is very convenient for students.
(v., n.)

decrease

2 Carol works a lot, so there is a _____ in the amount
(v., n.)

of her free time. She's not happy about this, but she

_____ the number of hours she works because she
(v., n.)

likes her job, too.

network

3 Ji Young regularly _____ with people in her field.
(v., n.)

She phones or e-mails at least four people a day. As a

result, she has a large _____ of people she can
(v., n.)

contact for work.

contact

4 Maria needs help with her visa, so she _____ the
(v., n.)

student advisor. He is an important _____ for all
(v., n.)

foreign students.

concern

⑤ Air pollution _____ me, so I walk to school instead of
(v., n.)

taking the bus. It's not a _____ for my roommate—
(v., n.)

he drives his car everywhere!

In English, verbs become nouns in several ways. Some verbs become nouns by adding the suffix –tion or –ation—for example, celebrate (v.) becomes celebration (n.), and participate (v.) becomes participation (n.). Complete each sentence with the correct form of the words on the left. **Use the correct tense of the verb in either the affirmative or the negative form.**

inform (v.)

information (n.)

① The teacher _____ the students about the final exam tomorrow. This _____ is very important.

compete (v.)

competition (n.)

② The Olympics is an international _____. People from all over the world _____ for gold, silver, and bronze medals.

communicate (v.)

communication (n.)

③ Peter _____ very well in English. As a result, _____ will be a problem when he visits the United States next month.

reduce (v.)

reduction (n.)

④ My doctor wants me to have a _____ in my weight, so I _____ the amount of sweets and ice cream that I eat from now on.

relax *(v.)*

relaxation *(n.)*

5 I enjoy going to the park for _____. It's very nice to sit under the trees and read a book. I _____ as much at home as I do in the park. It's much quieter in the park!

Word Partnership	Use *relax* with:
v.	**sit back and** relax
	begin to relax, **try to** relax
n.	**time to** relax
	relax *your* **body, muscles** relax

G Vocabulary in Context

access *(n.)*	**concerns** *(v.)*	**technology** *(n.)*
boundless *(adj.)*	**reduction** *(n.)*	**thrilled** *(adj.)*
communicate *(v.)*	**relax** *(v.)*	
compete *(v.)*	**solitary** *(adj.)*	

Read the following sentences. Complete each blank space with the correct word from the list above. Use each word only once.

1 Trudy is a very _____ person. She spends most of her time alone.

2 Parents and children don't always _____ very well, especially if they don't talk with each other enough.

3 Olga was accepted to the university of her choice. She is _____!

4 In order to have _____ to the library, you need to register and get a library card.

5 Simon and his brother always _____ with each other. Each one tries to be better than the other.

6 After class, Gloria and her friends _____ in the cafeteria together. They eat lunch and tell each other stories.

7 A typewriter is very simple _____, while a computer is very complex.

8 When William's first baby was born, his joy was _____. He was so happy and excited that he couldn't sleep.

9 After a holiday, there will often be a big _____ in prices. You can save a lot of money if you shop then.

10 Jason spends 6 hours a day at his computer. This _____ his parents. They worry that he doesn't get enough exercise.

H Critical Thinking Strategies

Read the following questions and think about the answers. Write your answer below each question. Then compare your answers with those of your classmates.

1 Michael Gilbert says, "It can't be a good thing that families are spending less face-to-face time together." What do you think happens when families spend less time together?

_____

_____

_____

_____

_____

2 Some people say that they communicate more with technology because they talk frequently with their cell phones, they send e-mail, and they use Facebook, Twitter, and MySpace.

    a. What are the advantages and disadvantages of communicating electronically with others, instead of communicating face-to-face?

        _____

        _____

        _____

    b. What conclusions can you make after thinking about these advantages and disadvantages?

        _____

        _____

        _____

I Topics for Discussion and Writing

1 Do you think families spend enough "face-to-face" time together? Why or why not? What might happen to families who don't spend a lot of time together?

2 Teachers sometimes complain that students spend so much time with technology that they do not read books any more. Teachers also say that students write less and are losing this skill. Is technology replacing books? Are students becoming poor writers?

3 **Write in your journal.** What effects has technology had on your life? How has it improved your life? Are there any negative effects of technology on your life?

Follow-Up Activities

How important are the following as sources of entertainment to you?

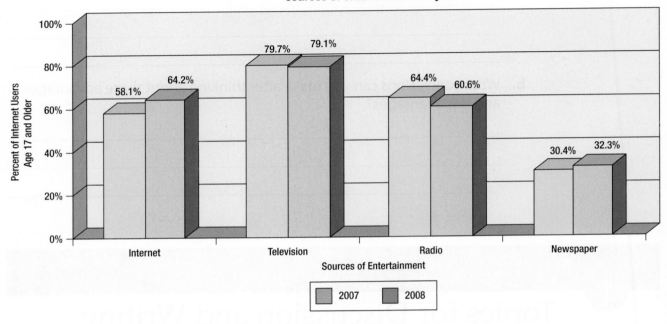

How important are the following as sources of entertainment to you?

Percent of Internet Users Age 17 and Older

Internet: 58.1% (2007), 64.2% (2008)
Television: 79.7% (2007), 79.1% (2008)
Radio: 64.4% (2007), 60.6% (2008)
Newspaper: 30.4% (2007), 32.3% (2008)

Sources of Entertainment

Legend: 2007, 2008

1 Look at the chart above, then read the following sentences. Circle the letter of each sentence that is true.

    a. The Internet was more important to people in 2007 than in 2008.

    b. Television was more important to people in 2007 than 2008.

    c. Radio was less important to people in 2008 than 2007.

    d. Newspapers were less important to people in 2007 than 2008.

    e. The Internet was more important than television in both years.

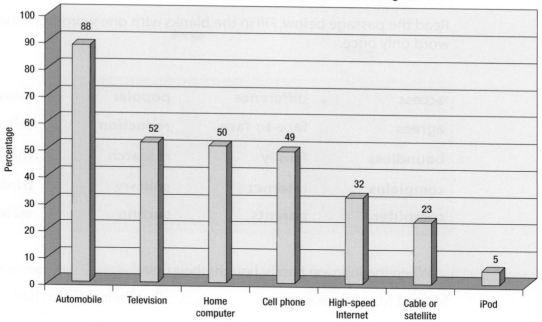

Percentage of Americans Who Say They Can't Live without These Technologies

Technology	Percentage
Automobile	88
Television	52
Home computer	50
Cell phone	49
High-speed Internet	32
Cable or satellite	23
iPod	5

2 Look at the chart above. Work in pairs. Which of the things on the chart are most important to you and your classmate? Put them in order on the chart below. #1 is the most important and #7 is the least important.

	Your Answers	Your Classmate's Answers
automobile	1.	1.
television set	2.	2.
home computer	3.	3.
cell phone	4.	4.
high-speed Internet	5.	5.
cable or satellite TV	6.	6.
iPod	7.	7.

Cloze Quiz

Read the passage below. Fill in the blanks with one word from the list. Use each word only once.

access	difference	popular	televisions
agrees	face-to-face	reduction	though
boundless	family	research	thrilled
complains	Internet	solitary	tripled
computer	parents	surfing	watching

When the Johnson family bought their first _____ several years ago, (1)

Mr. and Mrs. Johnson were _____ that their children had _____ (2) (3)

to so much information through the _____. Now, _____, they're (4) (5)

not as excited anymore. "Our family spends more time _____ the (6)

Internet than communicating with each other," _____ Mr. Johnson. The (7)

Johnson family is not alone in this situation. According to _____ by the (8)

Annenberg Center for the Digital Future at the University of Southern California,

in 2006, 11% of Americans said they were spending less time with their families.

Last year, the number almost _____ to 28%. (9)

It seems that as Internet use becomes more _____ (10), the amount of family time decreases. Many parents are concerned about this _____ (11) in the time their families spend together, and Michael Gilbert _____ (12). He is a researcher at the Annenberg Center. "Most people think of the Internet and our digital future as _____ (13) —unlimited—, and I do too," Gilbert said. However, he added, "It can't be a good thing that families are spending less _____ (14) time together."

As technology becomes more advanced, it often changes the ways that families interact. This is not a new concern. When _____ (15) first became popular in the 1950s, parents worried that their children were _____ (16) too much TV and spending too little time talking with their _____ (17). However, there is a significant _____ (18) between these two activities. Watching TV can be done as a _____ (19), while surfing the Internet is often a _____ (20) activity.

Crossword Puzzle

Crossword Puzzle Clues

3. Although
6. I come _____ class on time every day.
7. I always _____ my coffee with sugar.
9. Amount
12. The past of **is**
14. Status; rank
16. Way of living
17. The opposite of **on**
20. Unlimited
22. On time
23. I wanted to go to the movies, but I stayed home and studied _____.
24. People in a new country need to _____, or change, to the different customs.
27. Worried
28. Kathy always _____ the Internet to shop for good prices on anything she wants to buy.

1. Completely
2. I have _____ to the Internet. I will find that information for you online.
4. _____, two, three, four
5. Alert
8. The opposite of **yes**
10. The opposite of **down**
11. Excited
13. It is a bad idea to _____ breakfast. You should eat breakfast.
15. If I hurt someone's feelings, I always _____. I always say that I am sorry.
18. Hurry
19. Decrease

20. Actions

21. However

25. Impolite

26. We _____ learning English.

UNIT 1 | DISCUSSION

1. The three chapters in this unit discuss customs and trends in living: being on time, changing lifestyles and eating habits, and the effects of technology on people's lives. Work in a group of three or four and discuss the following questions.

    a. How do these topics describe cultures all over the world? Do people in all countries have these experiences?

    _____

    _____

    _____

    b. Think about these customs and trends in your own culture. Do people in your country feel the same about these features as Americans do? What would you say is important to the people in your culture?

    _____

    _____

    _____

2. Is there anything about your behavior or lifestyle that you might change after reading these chapters? If so, what?

    _____

    _____

    _____

4
CHAPTER

Language: Is It Always Spoken?

American Manual Alphabet

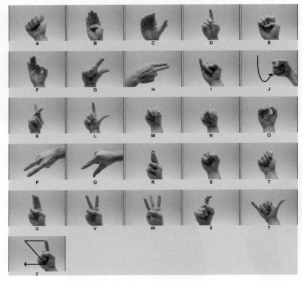

Prereading Preparation

1. What is language?
   a. Work with two partners and write a definition of the word **language** in the box below.
   b. Write your group's definition of **language** on the board. Compare your definition with your classmates' definitions.
   c. Look up the word **language** in your dictionary, and compare it to your definition.

Your Group's Definition	The Dictionary Definition

2. At what age do most babies learn to speak? How do they learn to speak?

3. How do you think deaf babies learn to communicate?

4. How do deaf people communicate?

5. Look at the American Manual Alphabet above. Who uses it and why?
   a. In groups of three, use the sign language chart to learn to "sign" an object in the room—for example, **chair** or **pen.**

b. Demonstrate your word to your classmates, and they will give the name of the object.

6 Read the title of this passage. Reread your definitions of **language**. Do you think human language must be spoken? Is there any other way that people can communicate?

Track 4

Language: Is It Always Spoken?

1   Most of us know a little about how babies learn to talk. From the time infants
2 are born, they hear language because their parents talk to them all the time.
3 Between the ages of seven and ten months, most infants begin to make sounds.
4 They repeat the same sounds over and over again. For example, a baby may
5 repeat the sound *"dadada"* or *"bababa."* This activity is called babbling. When
6 babies babble, they are practicing their language. Soon, the sound *"dadada"* may
7 become *"daddy,"* and *"bababa"* may become *"bottle."*
8   What happens, though, to children who cannot hear? How do deaf children
9 learn to communicate? Recently, doctors have learned that deaf babies babble
10 with their hands. Laura Ann Petitto, a psychologist at McGill University in
11 Montreal, Canada, has studied how children learn language. She observed
12 three hearing infants and two deaf infants. The three hearing infants had
13 English-speaking parents. The two deaf infants had deaf mothers and fathers
14 who used American Sign Language (ASL) to communicate with each other
15 and with their babies. Dr. Petitto studied the babies three times: at 10, 12,
16 and 14 months. During this time, children really begin to develop their
17 language skills.
18   After watching and videotaping the children for several hundred hours,
19 the psychologist and her assistants made many important observations. For
20 example, they saw that the hearing children made many different, varied
21 motions with their hands. However, there appeared to be no pattern to these
22 motions. The deaf babies also made many different movements with their
23 hands, but these movements were more consistent and deliberate. The deaf
24 babies seemed to make the same hand movements over and over again. During
25 the four-month period, the deaf babies' hand motions started to resemble some
26 of the basic hand-shapes used in ASL. The children also seemed to prefer certain
27 hand-shapes.

28   Hearing infants start first with simple syllable babbling (*dadada*), then put
29 more syllables together to sound like real sentences and questions. Apparently,
30 deaf babies follow this same pattern, too. First, they repeat simple hand-shapes.
31 Next, they form some simple hand signs (words) and use these movements
32 together to resemble ASL sentences.

33   Linguists—people who study language—believe that our ability for
34 language is innate. In other words, humans are born with the capacity
35 for language. It does not matter if we are physically able to speak or not.
36 Language can be expressed in many different ways—for instance, by speech
37 or by sign. Dr. Petitto believes this theory and wants to prove it. She plans to
38 study hearing children who have one deaf parent and one hearing parent.
39 Dr. Petitto wants to see what happens when babies have the opportunity to
40 learn both sign language and speech. Does the human brain prefer speech?
41 Some of these studies of hearing babies who have one deaf parent and one
42 hearing parent show that the babies babble equally with their hands and their
43 voices. They also produce their first words, both spoken and signed, at about
44 the same time.

45   The capacity for language is uniquely human. More studies in the future may
46 prove that the sign system of the deaf is the physical equivalent of speech. If so,
47 the old theory that only the spoken word is language will have to be changed.
48 The whole concept of human communication will have a very new and different
49 meaning.

UNIT 2   ISSUES IN SOCIETY

Fact-Finding Exercise

Read the passage again. Read the following statements. Check whether they are True or False. If a statement is false, rewrite the statement so that it is true. Then go back to the passage and find the line that supports your answer.

1 _____ True _____ False   Most infants start to babble before they are a year old.

_____

2 _____ True _____ False   Dr. Petitto studied only deaf babies.

_____

3 _____ True _____ False   The psychologist saw that deaf babies and hearing babies moved their hands the same way.

_____

4 _____ True _____ False   Dr. Petitto believes that we are all born with the ability for language.

_____

5 _____ True _____ False   Dr. Petitto believes that hearing babies who have one deaf parent and one hearing parent produce their first spoken words before their first signed words.

_____

Reading Analysis

Read each question carefully. Circle the letter or the number of the correct answer, or write your answer in the space provided.

1   What is the main idea of the passage?
   a. Both deaf children and hearing children learn to communicate in similar ways at about the same time.
   b. Children begin to develop their language skills at around two years of age.
   c. Many linguists believe that all humans are born with the ability to speak.

2   Read lines 3–5. What is **babbling?**

   _____

3   Read lines 13–15.
   a. What is **ASL?**

   _____

   b. Who uses ASL? Why?

   _____

4   Read lines 18 and 19. What is an **observation?**
   a. Something you see or hear
   b. Something you write
   c. Something important

5   In lines 19–21, what are **varied motions?**
   a. Different sounds
   b. Different movements
   c. Different signs

6   Read lines 20–24: ". . . they saw that the hearing children made many different, varied motions with their hands. However, there appeared to be no pattern to these motions. The deaf babies also made many different movements with their hands, but these movements were more consistent and deliberate. The deaf babies seemed to make the same hand movements over and over again."

a. Which of the following statements are true?

    1. All children make motions with their hands.
    2. Only the deaf children made many different movements with their hands.
    3. The hearing children's hand movements had a pattern.
    4. The deaf children's hand movements had a pattern.

b. Complete the following sentence correctly.

Both the deaf and the hearing children made movements with their hands, but

    1. only the hearing children made different movements
    2. they all made the same movements over and over again
    3. only the deaf children repeated the same hand motions
    4. only the hearing children repeated the same hand motions

7 Read lines 24–26: "During the four-month period, the deaf babies' hand motions started to resemble some of the basic hand-shapes used in ASL." This sentence means that

    a. the deaf babies were studying ASL
    b. the deaf babies were repeating their parents' hand signs
    c. the deaf babies stopped babbling

8 Read lines 33–35: "Linguists—people who study language—believe that our ability for language is innate. In other words, humans are born with the capacity for language."

    a. What is a **linguist?**

    _____

    b. How do you know?

    _____

    c. What does **capacity** mean?
        1. Language
        2. Ability
        3. Belief

    d. What does **innate** mean?

        1. Something you are born with
        2. Something you are able to do
        3. Something a linguist believes

e. What follows **in other words?**

    1. A new idea
    2. An explanation of the previous idea
    3. An example of the previous idea

9 Read lines 36 and 37.

  a. What are some different ways we can express language?

_____

  b. What does **for instance** mean?

    1. However
    2. So that
    3. For example

10 Read lines 45–47.

If so means

  a. if everyone agrees
  b. if this is true

C Information Organization

Read the passage again. Underline what you think are the main ideas. Then scan the reading and complete the following outline about the reading. Use the sentences that you have underlined to help you. You will use this outline later to answer questions about the reading.

  I. How Babies Learn Language
    A. Hearing Babies

      1. _____

        _____

      2. _____

B. Deaf Babies

1. _____

_____

2. _____

_____

II. Experiment on How Babies Learn Language

A. Who Conducted the Experiment:

_____

B. Who She Studied:

_____

C. How She Studied Them:

_____

D. Conclusion:

_____

_____

III. Future Experiments

A. Theory:

_____

B. Who She Will Study:

_____

C. Purpose of the Experiment:

_____

Information Recall and Summary

Read each question carefully. Use your outline to answer the questions. Do not refer back to the passage. When you are finished, write a brief summary of the reading.

1   **a.** What is babbling?

_____

       b. When does it occur?

_____

2   Who did Dr. Petitto study? Why?

_____

_____

3   What did the psychologist and her assistants discover after they watched the videotapes of the children?

_____

_____

_____

4   What theory does Dr. Petitto believe about language learning?

_____

5   Who does this psychologist want to study next? Why?

_____

_____

Summary

Work in pairs or alone. Write a brief summary of the reading, and put it on the board. Compare your summary with your classmates'. Which one best describes the main idea of the reading?

_____

_____

_____

E Dictionary Skills

Read the following sentences. Use the context to help you understand the boldface words. Read the dictionary entry for that word and circle the appropriate definition. Then choose the sentence with the correct answer.

1. **pattern** *n.* **1** an example or model to be followed: *A research paper must follow a specific pattern.* **2** a form or guide to follow when making s.t.: *She made the dress herself from a pattern.* **3** a design of regular shapes and lines: *The flower pattern in that dress is very pretty.* **4** a repeated set of events, characteristics, or features: *There is a pattern to his behavior, in that he grows quiet when he's sad.*

   —*v.* [T] to make by following a pattern: *She patterned her wedding dress after her mother's.* || *He patterns himself after his father, who is athletic and very serious.*

   They saw that the hearing children made many different, varied motions with their hands. However, there appeared to be no **pattern** to these motions.

   a. There appeared to be no model to follow in these motions.
   b. There appeared to be no repeated set of characteristics in these motions.
   c. There appeared to be no design of regular shapes and lines in these motions.
   d. There appeared to be no form or guide to follow when making these motions.

2. **capacity** *n.* -ties **1** *sing.* [U] the ability to contain, hold, or absorb: *That restaurant has a 100-seat capacity.* **2** *sing.* [U] the greatest amount that s.t. can contain, the maximum volume: *There is no more room in the bottle; it is filled to capacity.* **3** [C; U] the ability to do s.t.: *He has the capacity to work long hours.* **4** [C; U] the power to learn and remember knowledge: *She has a great capacity for learning.* **5** [C] the power that goes with a certain position or role: *She signs the company checks in her capacity as owner.* **6** [U] the best or maximum amount of production: *That factory is working at capacity.*

   The **capacity** for language is uniquely human.

   a. The greatest amount of language that can be contained is uniquely human.
   b. The ability to contain or hold language is uniquely human.
   c. The power to learn and remember language is uniquely human.

F

Word Forms

In English, adjectives change to nouns in several ways. Some adjectives become nouns by changing the final *-t* to *-ce*—for example, *ignorant (adj.)* becomes *ignorance (n.)*. Complete each sentence with the correct form of the words on the left. **Use the singular or plural form of the noun.**

important *(adj.)*

importance *(n.)*

(1) Whether you write a composition with a pen or pencil is of very little _____. What is much more _____ is the content of the composition.

different *(adj.)*

difference *(n.)*

(2) Some languages aren't very _____ from each other, for example, Spanish and Portuguese. Other languages, however, have significant _____, for example, Chinese and Russian.

significant *(adj.)*

significance *(n.)*

(3) The introduction of the personal computer in 1980 had _____ effects on our everyday lives. We can understand the unbelievable _____ of this machine when we realize that today there are tens of millions of PCs in the United States alone.

dependent *(adj.)*

dependence *(n.)*

(4) As children grow up, their _____ on their parents decreases. However, children usually remain financially _____ on their parents for many years.

persistent (adj.)

persistence (n.)

⑤ Rebecca is an incredibly _____ person. She studied hard for four years to get a scholarship to college. As a result of her _____, she did well on her tests and got a scholarship to a good university.

In English, verbs change to nouns in several ways. Some verbs become nouns by adding the suffix -ing—for example, *learn (v.)* becomes *learning (n.)*. Complete each sentence with the correct form of the words on the left. **Use the correct tense of the verb in either the affirmative or the negative form. Use the singular or plural form of the noun.**

talk (v.)

talking (n.)

① For most people, _____ is an important social activity. Unfortunately, some people _____ too much.

begin (v.)

beginning (n.)

② Harry needs to rewrite his composition. He _____ each paragraph with an indentation, but he should have. A composition needs an indentation at the _____ of every paragraph.

hear (v.)

hearing (n.)

③ The school nurse checks the _____ of all the students in every class. If a child _____ well, the nurse informs the parents and suggests that they take their child to a doctor.

babble (v.)

babbling (n.)

④ Rod and Cheryl's baby _____ all the time. They are very excited about her _____ because she is saying "*mamma*" and "*dada*."

mean (v.)

meaning (n.)

5 The verb *get* _____ so many different things that I sometimes have trouble understanding it in a sentence. The word *get* has so many different _____ that I become confused about using it, too.

Word Partnership	Use *meaning* with:
n.	meaning **of a term**, meaning **of a word**
adj.	**literal** meaning, **deeper** meaning, **new** meaning, **real** meaning
v.	**explain the** meaning **of** *something*, **understand the** meaning **of** *something*

G Vocabulary in Context

capacity (n.)	in other words	persistent (adj.)
for instance	meaning (n.)	varied (adj.)
if so	motion (n.)	
innate (adj.)	observation (n.)	

Read the following sentences. Complete each blank space with the correct word or phrase from the list above. Use each word or phrase only once.

1 Eugene is a very _____ student. He never stops working until he finishes a job, regardless of how difficult it is for him.

2 It may rain on Saturday. _____, we won't go on a picnic. We'll see a movie instead.

3 If Jackie doesn't understand the _____ of a word from the context, she uses her English dictionary.

4 Animals do not have the _____ for speech. Only humans can communicate with language.

5 Henry has a _____ life. During the day, he is a student. In the evenings, he works as a waiter. On Saturdays, he teaches swimming to children, and on Sundays, he sings in a choir.

6 Researchers have to have training in _____. They need to learn what to look for and how to record what they see.

7 Human babies have many _____ abilities. Walking and speaking are two of them.

8 In different cultures, the same _____, such as waving your hand, may have different meanings.

9 Janet complains about everything. She's always too warm or too cold. She doesn't like anything. _____ Janet is a very negative person.

10 Matthew enjoys going out to restaurants to experience eating the food of different cultures. _____, one month he will go to an Indian restaurant. Then he will try Japanese food. After that, he will go to a Colombian or a Greek restaurant.

Critical Thinking Strategies

Read the following questions and think about the answers. Write your answer below each question. Then compare your answers with those of your classmates.

1 Dr. Petitto studied the babies at 10 months, 12 months and 14 months. Why do you think she studied them so often?

_____

_____

2 Doctors recently learned that deaf babies "babble" with their hands. How do you think they do this?

_____

_____

Topics for Discussion and Writing

1 Many famous people of the past and present have been deaf. Despite their disability, they were successful in their lives. For example, Helen Keller was an important author and scholar, and Marlee Matlin is a famous American actress. What other famous people do you know who were or are hearing-impaired (deaf)? Write about one of these people. Tell about what that person has accomplished in spite of his or her disability.

2 Sign language is one important form of nonverbal communication. Can you think of another type of nonverbal communication? Describe it.

3 **Write in your journal.** Is it important for you to learn sign language? Why or why not?

Follow-Up Activities

J

1. Doctors have developed a controversial operation (a cochlear implant) to enable the deaf to "hear." Many deaf people are opposed to this operation. They say that they are not really disabled. They feel they are a minority group and should be accepted as they are—non-hearing people. They feel it is wrong to force children to have this operation and that the operation does not really enable the deaf to hear as well as non-deaf people do anyway. They feel that their sign language should be accepted as any spoken language is.

   Work in a group of four. Make a list of the advantages and disadvantages of remaining deaf (and not having the operation) and the advantages and disadvantages of having the operation. Next to your list of advantages and disadvantages, write the consequences of remaining deaf and the consequences of being able to "hear." Compare your list with your classmates' lists.

2. Many deaf people feel that ASL is a real language. They believe that hearing people should learn it just as they learn other languages. The American Manual Alphabet on page 58 is only for spelling out words, letter by letter. Go to the library and find a book on learning ASL. In small groups, learn to "sign" some basic rules and sentences. Then, in your group, discuss what it may be like to learn ASL, compared to learning a spoken language. Discuss your conclusions with your classmates.

Cloze Quiz

Read the passage below. Fill in the blanks with one word from the list. Use each word only once.

babies	innate	observations	resemble
capacity	language	over	same
consistent	learn	pattern	speech
deaf	matter	prefer	varied
example	movements	psychologist	words

Recently, doctors have learned that deaf _____ babble with their hands.
(1)
Laura Ann Petitto, a _____ at McGill University in Montreal, Canada, has
(2)
studied how children _____ language. She observed three hearing infants
(3)
and two _____ infants. After watching and videotaping the children for
(4)
several hundred hours, the psychologist and her assistants made many important
_____. For _____, they saw that the hearing children made many
(5)   (6)
different, _____ motions with their hands. However, there appeared to
(7)
be no _____ to these motions. The deaf babies also made many different
(8)
_____ with their hands, but these movements were more _____
(9)   (10)
and deliberate. The deaf babies seemed to make the _____ hand
(11)
movements over and _____ again. During the four-month period, the
(12)
deaf babies' hand motions started to _____ some of the basic hand-shapes
(13)
used in ASL. The children also seemed to _____ certain hand-shapes.
(14)

Linguists—people who study language—believe that our ability for
language is _____. In other _____, humans are born with the
(15)   (16)
_____ for language. It does not _____ if we are physically able
(17)   (18)
to speak or not. _____ can be expressed in many different ways—for
(19)
instance, by _____ or by sign.
(20)

5 CHAPTER

Loneliness: How Can We Overcome It?

Prereading Preparation

1 What is **loneliness?**

_____

_____

_____

2 Are **loneliness** and being **alone** the same? Why or why not?

_____

_____

_____

3 Look at the table at the top of page 76. Work with a partner and make a list of some reasons why people may feel lonely. Have you or your partner ever felt lonely for these reasons? Discuss your answers with your classmate.

4 Do you think everyone feels lonely at some time in his or her life? Do you think this is common? Explain your answer.

_____

_____

_____

_____

_____

Reasons People Feel Lonely	You	Your Partner
1.	yes / no	yes / no
2.	yes / no	yes / no
3.	yes / no	yes / no
4.	yes / no	yes / no
5.	yes / no	yes / no

5 How would you answer the question in the title of this chapter?

_____

_____

Track 5

Loneliness: How Can We Overcome It?

1   Most people feel lonely sometimes, but it usually only lasts between a few
2   minutes and a few hours. This kind of loneliness is not serious. In fact, it is quite
3   normal. For some people, though, loneliness can last for years. Psychologists are
4   studying this complex phenomenon in an attempt to better understand long-
5   term loneliness. These researchers have already identified three different types
6   of loneliness.
7   The first kind of loneliness is temporary. This is the most common type. It
8   usually disappears quickly and does not require any special attention. The
9   second kind, situational loneliness, is a natural result of a particular situation—
10 for example, a divorce, the death of a loved one, or moving to a new place.
11 Although this kind of loneliness can cause physical problems, such as headaches
12 and sleeplessness, it usually does not last for more than a year. Situational
13 loneliness is easy to understand and to predict.

14   The third kind of loneliness is the most severe. Unlike the second type,
15 chronic loneliness usually lasts more than two years and has no specific cause.
16 People who experience habitual loneliness have problems socializing and
17 becoming close to others. Unfortunately, many chronically lonely people think
18 there is little or nothing they can do to improve their condition.

19   Psychologists agree that one important factor in loneliness is a person's
20 social contacts, e.g., friends, family members, coworkers, etc. We depend on
21 various people for different reasons. For instance, our families give us emotional
22 support, our parents and teachers give us guidance, and our friends share
23 similar interests and activities. However, psychologists have found that the
24 number of social contacts we have is not the only reason for loneliness. It is more
25 important how many social contacts we think or expect we should have. In other
26 words, though lonely people may have many social contacts, they sometimes
27 feel they should have more. They question their own popularity.

28   Most researchers agree that the loneliest people are between the ages of 18 and
29 25, so a group of psychologists decided to study a group of college freshmen.
30 They found that more than 50% of the freshmen were situationally lonely at the
31 beginning of the semester as a result of their new circumstances, but had adjusted
32 after a few months. Thirteen percent were still lonely after seven months due
33 to shyness and fear. They felt very uncomfortable meeting new people, even
34 though they understood that their fear was not rational. The situationally lonely
35 freshmen overcame their loneliness by making new friends, but the chronically
36 lonely remained unhappy because they were afraid to do so.

37	Psychologists are trying to find ways to help habitually lonely people for
38	two reasons. First of all, they are unhappy and unable to socialize. Secondly,
39	researchers have found a connection between chronic loneliness and serious
40	illnesses such as heart disease. While temporary and situational loneliness
41	can be a normal, healthy part of life, chronic loneliness can be a very sad, and
42	sometimes dangerous, condition.

A Fact-Finding Exercise

Read the passage again. Read the following statements. Check whether they are True or False. If a statement is false, rewrite the statement so that it is true. Then go back to the passage and find the line that supports your answer.

1 _____ True _____ False Psychologists say there are two different kinds of loneliness.

_____

2 _____ True _____ False All kinds of loneliness last only a short time.

_____

3 _____ True _____ False Temporary loneliness is very serious.

_____

4 _____ True _____ False Divorce sometimes causes loneliness.

_____

5 _____ True _____ False Loneliness can cause sleeplessness and headaches.

_____

6 _____ True _____ False Chronic loneliness usually lasts more than two years.

_____

7 _____ True _____ False   Lonely people have no social contacts.

_____

8 _____ True _____ False   The loneliest people are over 50 years old.

_____

9 _____ True _____ False   Chronic loneliness can cause serious illness.

_____

B Reading Analysis

Read each question carefully. Circle the letter or the number of the correct answer, or write your answer in the space provided.

1 What is the main idea of the passage?
  a. There are three kinds of loneliness.
  b. Chronic loneliness is the most severe kind.
  c. Researchers want to cure loneliness.

2 Read lines 3 and 4.
  a. What does **last** mean?
    1. Finish
    2. Hurt
    3. Continue

  b. What does **this complex phenomenon** refer to?
    1. Loneliness that lasts for years
    2. Loneliness that lasts for hours

3 Read lines 14–17.
  a. What does **unlike** show?
    1. A similarity
    2. A difference
    3. An addition

b. Which word in these sentences is a synonym for **chronic?**

_____

4 Read lines 19 and 20.

  a. What follows **e.g.?**

   1. Examples
   2. Proof
   3. Explanations

  b. What does **etc.** mean?

   1. For example
   2. And others
   3. End of sentence

5 In line 21, **for instance** introduces

  a. explanations
  b. examples
  c. results

6 Read lines 25–27. How does **in other words** help you?

_____

7 In line 27, what does **question** mean?

  a. Ask a question
  b. Have doubts about

8 Read lines 34–36.

  a. What does "the situationally lonely freshmen overcame their loneliness" mean?

   1. They accepted their loneliness.
   2. They were no longer lonely.
   3. They made new friends.

  b. What does ". . . they were afraid to do so" mean?

_____

9 Read lines 40–42. What does **while** mean?

  a. At the same time
  b. During
  c. Although

Information Organization

Read the passage again. Underline what you think are the main ideas. Then scan the reading and complete the following flowchart, using the sentences that you have underlined to help you. You will use this flowchart later to answer questions about the reading.

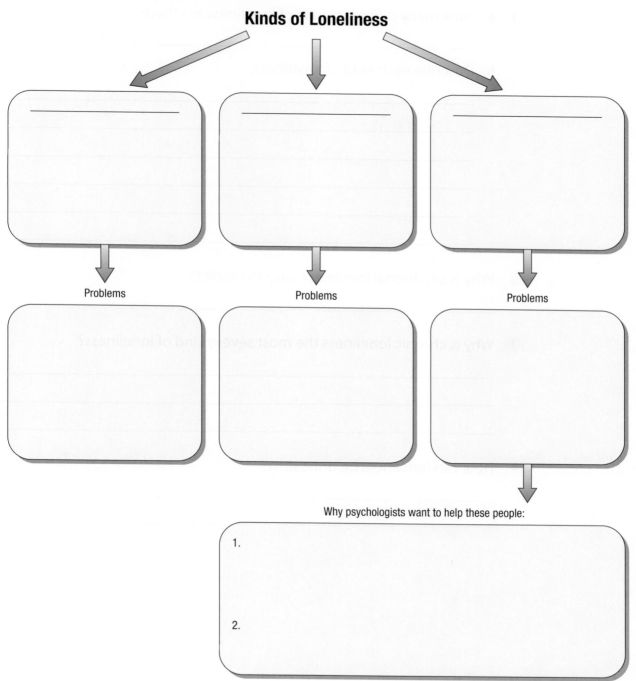

Kinds of Loneliness

Problems

Problems

Problems

Why psychologists want to help these people:

1.

2.

Information Recall and Summary

Read each question carefully. Use your flowchart to answer the questions. Do not refer back to the passage. When you are finished, write a brief summary of the reading.

1 a. How many different kinds of loneliness are there?

_____

b. Describe each kind of loneliness.

_____

_____

_____

_____

_____

_____

2 Why is situational loneliness easy to predict?

_____

3 Why is chronic loneliness the most severe kind of loneliness?

_____

_____

_____

4 How can loneliness be unhealthy?

_____

_____

Summary

Work in pairs or alone. Write a brief summary of the reading, and put it on the board. Compare your summary with your classmates'. Which one best describes the main idea of the reading?

_____

_____

_____

Dictionary Skills

Read the following sentences. Use the context to help you understand the boldface words. Read the dictionary entry for that word and circle the appropriate definition. Then choose the sentence with the correct answer.

1.
> **factor** *n.* **1** a fact to be considered: *The high cost of labor is an important factor in the price of steel.* **2** a number by which a larger number can be divided: *Two and four are factors of eight.*

Psychologists agree that one important **factor** in loneliness is a person's social contacts, e.g., friends, family, coworkers, etc.

a. Psychologists agree that one important organization doing business to be considered in loneliness is a person's social contacts, e.g., friends, family, coworkers, etc.

b. Psychologists agree that one important number by which another number can be divided in loneliness is a person's social contacts, e.g., friends, family, coworkers, etc.

c. Psychologists agree that one important fact to be considered in loneliness is a person's social contacts, e.g., friends, family, coworkers, etc.

2.
> **contact** *n.* **1** [U] touch: *My clothes come in contact with my skin.* **2** [C] a person one knows, esp. who can get s.t. done: *She has contacts with top officials in the government.* **3** [C] an electrical point: *The contact on the car battery is broken.* **4** communication with s.o.: *He made contact by telephone with his friend.*

Psychologists have found that the number of social **contacts** we have is not the only reason for loneliness.

   a. Psychologists have found that the number of people we know who can get something done is not the only reason for loneliness.
   b. Psychologists have found that the amount of communication we have with others is not the only reason for loneliness.
   c. Psychologists have found that the number of electrical points we have with others is not the only reason for loneliness.

3 | **question** *v.* [T] **1** to look for an answer to s.t. unknown or in doubt: *She questioned the teacher about a difficult problem.* **2** to try to get information from s.o.: *The police questioned the prisoner.* **3** to wonder if s.t. is just, good, or legal: *Some people question the legality of that government.*

Lonely people sometimes feel they should have more friends. They **question** their own popularity.

   a. Lonely people sometimes feel they should have more friends. They try to get information from others about their popularity.
   b. Lonely people sometimes feel they should have more friends. They are in doubt about their popularity.
   c. Lonely people sometimes feel they should have more friends. They wonder if they are popular enough.

F Word Forms

PART 1

In English, adjectives become nouns in several ways. Some adjectives become nouns by adding the suffix -*ness*—for example, *sick (adj.)* becomes *sickness (n.)*. Complete each sentence with the correct form of the words on the left.

happy *(adj.)*   **1** My nieces are very _____ children. Their

happiness *(n.)*   _____ is important to my sister and

her husband.

ill *(adj.)*

illness *(n.)*

(2) The teacher left school early because she felt
_____ during class. Fortunately, her
_____ seemed to improve by the next morning.

lonely *(adj.)*

loneliness *(n.)*

(3) My aunt overcame her _____ by going out more
often with her friends. She was very _____ after
her husband died.

shy *(adj.)*

shyness *(n.)*

(4) Some doctors think that _____ children are born
that way. This _____ often prevents them from
doing well in school.

sleepless *(adj.)*

sleeplessness *(n.)*

(5) My father finally went to the doctor because his
_____ was so severe. After several _____
nights, he was exhausted.

PART 2

In English, some adjectives become nouns by adding the suffix -*ity*—for example,
national (adj.) becomes *nationality (n.)*. Complete each sentence with the correct
form of the words on the left. **Use the singular or plural form of the noun.**

complex *(adj.)*

complexity *(n.)*

(1) The _____ of math depends on the type of
math. For example, arithmetic is very simple. In contrast,
calculus is a very _____ subject.

popular *(adj.)*

popularity *(n.)*

(2) One of the most _____ fast foods in the United
States is the hamburger. Its incredible _____ will
probably continue for many years.

similar *(adj.)*

similarity *(n.)*

(3) England and the United States are _____ because
the people speak the same language. However, culturally,
there are fewer _____ and many differences.

rational (adj.)
rationality (n.)

4 Under ordinary circumstances, most people act in a _____ manner. Under unusual circumstances, however, many people's level of _____ decreases.

equal (adj.)
equality (n.)

5 The American Constitution guarantees _____ to everyone under the law. In other words, every person living in the United States has _____ rights.

Word Partnership	Use *equal* with:
n.	equal **importance**, equal **number**, equal **parts**, equal **pay**, equal **share**, equal **rights**, equal **treatment**

G Vocabulary in Context

chronic (adj.)	**predicted** (v.)	**temporary** (adj.)
factors (n.)	**remain** (v.)	**unlike** (adj.)
for instance	**severe** (adj.)	
overcame (v.)	**shy** (adj.)	

Read the following sentences. Complete each blank space with the correct word or phrase from the list above. Use each word or phrase only once.

1 Helen is very thin, _____ her sister, who is quite heavy.

2 After I learn English, I will _____ in this country and get a good job.

3 This beautiful weather is only _____. It is going to rain for the rest of this week.

4 Artie finally _____ his fear of flying when he went to Florida by plane.

5 I am always waiting for Debbie because she is late for everything. Her _____ lateness is destroying our friendship.

6 Yolanda is a _____ student. She is very quiet and always sits alone in class.

7 This morning, the newscaster _____ snow for tomorrow.

8 My uncle went to the hospital because he suddenly had a _____ pain in his back.

9 A proper diet and frequent exercise are important _____ in maintaining good health.

10 Barbara has many varied interests. _____, she enjoys music, horseback riding, and coin collecting.

Critical Thinking Strategies

Read the following questions and think about the answers. Write your answer below each question. Then compare your answers with those of your classmates.

1 Many lonely people have a lot of social contacts, but they feel they should have more. Why do you think they feel this way?

_____

_____

_____

2 Why do you think the loneliest people are between the ages of 18 and 25? What do you think are some reasons for their loneliness?

_____

_____

_____

I

Topics for Discussion and Writing

1 In this article, the author states that young adults (18 to 25 years old) are the loneliest people in the United States. Think about this statement. What do you think may be some reasons for this?

2 Do you think it is important for psychologists and researchers to study loneliness? Why or why not?

3 **Write in your journal.** Describe a time in your life when you felt lonely. What did you do to overcome your loneliness?

Follow-Up Activity

In the article, the author states that in the United States, the loneliest people are young adults (18 to 25 years old). Is this also true in your country? Are different people lonely in different cultures? Take a survey in your class. Ask your classmates who the loneliest people are in their cultures. Then put the results of the survey on the board. With your classmates, discuss what you think are the reasons for these results.

Country	Loneliest Age	Possible Reasons
U.S.A.	18–25	Many young people are in college and away from home.

Cloze Quiz

Read the passage below. Fill in the blanks with one word from the list. Use each word only once.

chronic	instance	phenomenon	severe
circumstances	interests	popularity	shyness
connection	loneliness	predict	temporary
factor	normal	rational	unfortunately
habitual	overcame	remained	words

Most people feel lonely sometimes, but it usually only lasts between a few minutes and a few hours. This kind of loneliness is not serious. In fact, it is quite _____. For some people, though, loneliness can last for years.
(1)
Psychologists are studying this complex _____ in an attempt to better
(2)
understand long-term loneliness. These researchers have already identified three different types of loneliness.

The first kind of loneliness is _____. This is the most common
(3)
type. It usually disappears quickly and does not require any special attention. The second kind, situational _____, is a natural result of a particular
(4)
situation—for example, a divorce, the death of a loved one, or moving to a new place. Although this kind of loneliness can cause physical problems, such as headaches and sleeplessness, it usually does not last for more than a year. Situational loneliness is easy to understand and to _____.
(5)

The third kind of loneliness is the most _____. Unlike the second
(6)
type, chronic loneliness usually lasts more than two years and has no specific cause. People who experience _____ loneliness have problems
(7)
socializing and becoming close to others. _____, many chronically lonely
(8)
people think there is little or nothing they can do to improve their condition.

Psychologists agree that one important _____ (9) in loneliness is a person's social contacts, e.g., friends, family members, coworkers, etc. We depend on various people for different reasons. For _____, (10) our families give us emotional support, our parents and teachers give us guidance, and our friends share similar _____ (11) and activities. However, psychologists have found that the number of social contacts we have is not the only reason for loneliness. It is more important how many social contacts we think or expect we should have. In other _____, (12) though lonely people may have many social contacts, they sometimes feel they should have more. They question their own _____. (13)

Most researchers agree that the loneliest people are between the ages of 18 and 25, so a group of psychologists decided to study a group of college freshmen. They found that more than 50% of the freshmen were situationally lonely at the beginning of the semester as a result of their new _____, (14) but had adjusted after a few months. Thirteen percent were still lonely after seven months due to _____ (15) and fear. They felt very uncomfortable meeting new people, even though they understood that their fear was not _____. (16) The situationally lonely freshmen _____ (17) their loneliness by making new friends, but the chronically lonely _____ (18) unhappy because they were afraid to do so.

Psychologists are trying to find ways to help habitually lonely people for two reasons. First of all, they are unhappy and unable to socialize. Secondly, researchers have found a _____ (19) between chronic loneliness and serious illnesses such as heart disease. While temporary and situational loneliness can be a normal, healthy part of life, _____ (20) loneliness can be a very sad, and sometimes dangerous, condition.

6

The Importance of Grandmothers

Prereading Preparation

1 Work in a small group. Talk about your grandmothers.

a. What memories do you have of them from your childhood? For example, what did you do when you were with your grandmothers? How did they treat you? What food or gifts did they give you?

b. Did both of your grandmothers always treat you the same? In what ways did one grandmother treat you differently from your other grandmother? Use the chart below to write your answers.

	My Father's Mother	My Mother's Mother
How did they treat you the same?		
How did they treat you differently?		

2 As a class, share your information about your grandmothers. Make a list on the board of all the students' responses. What differences are there between your fathers' mothers and your mothers' mothers?

3 Read the title of this passage. What do you think you are going to read about?

Track 6

The Importance of Grandmothers

1   What do you think of when you think about your grandmothers? Many
2   people have happy memories of their grandmothers. Their grandmothers loved
3   them, paid attention to them, and gave them special treats, such as toys and
4   sweets. Sometimes, grandmothers even helped them when they had problems
5   with their parents. It seems that for many people, their grandmothers were a
6   very happy part of their childhood.
7   In recent years, anthropologists have begun to study the role of grandmothers.
8   Anthropologists are scientists who study people, societies, and cultures. They
9   studied infants and children to learn about the factors that helped infants
10 and children survive. Anthropologists usually looked at parents and did not
11 pay much attention to grandparents. However, now they are studying how
12 grandmothers also influence the survival rate of their grandchildren.
13   Many biologists and anthropologists now believe that the role of grandmothers
14 in a family is very important. Grandmothers may be the reason why human
15 infants, who take so many years to grow up, are able to survive. The biologists
16 and anthropologists are starting to examine grandmothers within different
17 societies and cultures. In fact, at one international conference, the role of
18 grandmothers was the main topic. The biologists and anthropologists explained
19 that although grandmothers no longer have children, many grandmothers are
20 still young and active. As a result, they have the time and energy to help with
21 their grandchildren. This extra help may be an important factor in reducing the
22 mortality, or death, rate among young children.
23   Some people at the conference studied different societies. They explained
24 that in many cultures, having a grandmother in the family made a significant
25 difference in the child's chances of living. In fact, the grandmother's presence
26 sometimes improved a child's chance of survival even more than the father's
27 presence did. In other words, it was sometimes more important for a child to
28 have a grandmother than for a child to have a father!

Dr. Ruth Mace and Dr. Rebecca Sear work in the Department of Anthropology at University College in London. They collected and studied information about people in the countryside in Gambia, Africa. At the time of their study, the child mortality rate was very high. Dr. Mace and Dr. Sear looked at children who were about one to three years old. They discovered that the presence or absence of the child's father did not affect the death rate. However, the presence of a grandmother reduced the children's chances of dying by 50%. These anthropologists made another discovery that surprised them very much. The children were only helped by the presence of their maternal grandmother— their mother's mother. The presence of their father's mother, or paternal grandmother, had no effect on the mortality rate.

Dr. Cheryl Jamison is an anthropologist at Indiana University in Bloomington. She worked with colleagues to study the population records of a village in central Japan for the period 1671 through 1871. They found that the mortality rate for children in the village was very high. In fact, 27.5% of children died by the age of 16. They then studied girl and boy children separately and looked for the presence of grandmothers. Again, the anthropologists were surprised by their discovery. The death rate for girls was not different whether or not a grandmother lived with them. However, there was a great difference in the survival rate of boys. If a maternal grandmother lived in the household, boys were 52% less likely to die in childhood. The anthropologists were very surprised to find that boys were 62% more likely to die in childhood when a paternal grandmother lived in the household. Dr. Jamison said that in this society, families usually lived with the husband's parents, so very few children lived with their maternal grandmothers.

Today, many children do not live with their grandmothers. However, grandmothers still have an important role in their grandchildren's lives. They still love and care for their grandchildren, and make their lives happier, too.

Fact-Finding Exercise

Read the passage again. Read the following statements. Check whether they are True or False. If a statement is false, rewrite the statement so that it is true. Then go back to the passage and find the line that supports your answer.

1 _____ True _____ False Anthropologists believe that grandmothers often help their grandchildren survive.

_____

2 _____ True _____ False Many grandmothers are too old to help with their grandchildren.

_____

3 _____ True _____ False Some people at the conference believe that having a grandmother in the family may reduce a child's survival rate.

_____

4 _____ True _____ False In Gambia, the presence of a father increased a child's survival rate.

_____

5 _____ True _____ False The death rate for girls in Japan decreased when the grandmother lived with the family.

_____

6 _____ True _____ False From 1671 to 1871, Japanese families usually lived with the husband's parents.

_____

7 _____ True _____ False The survival rate for boys in Japan increased when the maternal grandmother lived in the household.

_____

Reading Analysis

Read each question carefully. Circle the letter or the number of the correct answer, or write your answer in the space provided.

1 What is the main idea of the passage?

   a. Maternal grandmothers always love their grandchildren more than paternal grandmothers do.

   b. In many cultures, grandmothers play an important role in the lives of their young grandchildren.

   c. Grandfathers play no role at all in the lives of their young grandchildren.

2 Read lines 2–4. What are **treats?**

   a. Toys

   b. Candy

   c. Small gifts

3 Read lines 5 and 6. When is a person's **childhood?**

   a. The period from birth to age 13

   b. The period from birth to age 21

   c. The period from birth to marriage

4 Read lines 7–12.

   a. What is an **anthropologist?**

   _____

   _____

   b. What is a **factor?**

     1. A parent or other relative

     2. Something that influences something else

     3. A danger to someone's life

   c. What does **influence** mean?

     1. Assist

     2. Affect

     3. Harm

5 Read lines 14–15. What does **survive** mean?

   a. Continue to live
   b. Be happy
   c. Depend on

6 Read lines 21 and 22.

   a. What does **reducing** mean?

   1. Helping
   2. Stopping
   3. Decreasing

   b. What does **mortality** mean?

   _____

   _____

   c. How do you know?

   _____

   _____

7 Read lines 21 and 22. **This extra help** means

   a. the grandmother's help
   b. the anthropologist's help
   c. the parents' help

8 Read lines 23–25. What does **significant** mean?

   a. Very positive
   b. Very negative
   c. Very important

9 Read lines 36–38.

   a. Which side of a person's family is the **maternal** side?

   1. The father's side
   2. The mother's side

b. Which side of a person's family is the **paternal** side?

    1. The father's side
    2. The mother's side

c. Your parents' brothers and sisters are your uncles and aunts. Specifically, your mother's brother is

    1. your maternal uncle
    2. your paternal uncle

d. Your father's sister is
    1. your maternal aunt
    2. your paternal aunt

10 Read lines 46–49. A **household** is

    a. the building that a family lives in together
    b. the people who live together in one home

Information Organization

Read the passage a second time. Underline what you think are the main ideas. Then scan the reading and complete the following outline, using the sentences that you have underlined to help you. You will use this outline later to answer questions about the reading.

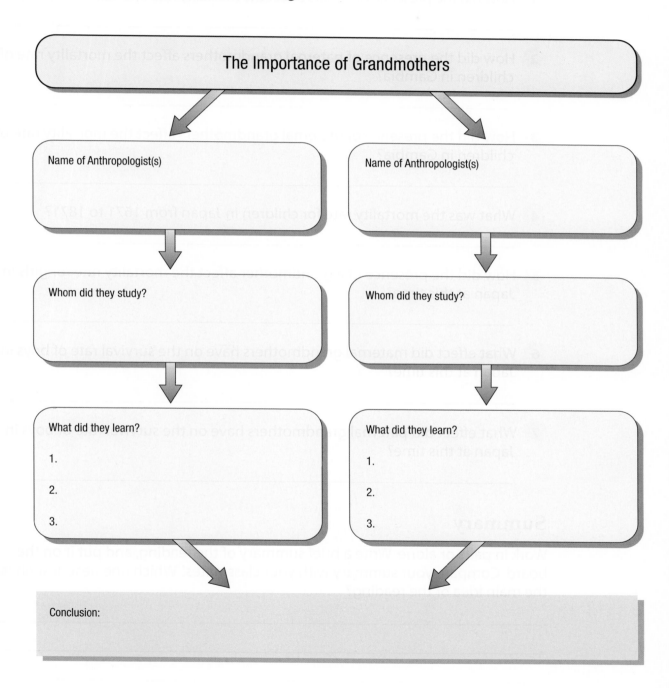

The Importance of Grandmothers

Name of Anthropologist(s)

Name of Anthropologist(s)

Whom did they study?

Whom did they study?

What did they learn?

1.

2.

3.

What did they learn?

1.

2.

3.

Conclusion:

Information Recall and Summary

Read each question carefully. Use your outline to answer the questions. Do not refer back to the passage. When you are finished, write a brief summary of the reading.

1 How did the presence of fathers affect the mortality rate of children in Gambia?

_____

2 How did the presence of paternal grandmothers affect the mortality rate of children in Gambia?

_____

3 How did the presence of maternal grandmothers affect the mortality rate of children in Gambia?

_____

4 What was the mortality rate for children in Japan from 1671 to 1871?

_____

5 How did the presence of a grandmother affect the mortality rate for girls in Japan at this time?

_____

6 What effect did maternal grandmothers have on the survival rate of boys in Japan at this time?

_____

7 What effect did paternal grandmothers have on the survival rate of boys in Japan at this time?

_____

Summary

Work in pairs or alone. Write a brief summary of the reading, and put it on the board. Compare your summary with your classmates'. Which one best describes the main idea of the reading?

_____

_____

_____

Dictionary Skills

Read the following sentences. Use the context to help you understand the boldface words. Read the dictionary entry for that word and circle the appropriate definition. Then choose the sentence with the correct answer.

1 | **culture** *n.* [C; U] **1** the ideas, activities (art, foods, businesses), and ways of behaving that are special to a country, people, or region: *In North American culture, men do not kiss men when meeting each other. They shake hands.* **2** [U] the achievements of a people or nation in art, music, literature, etc.: *The Chinese have had a high culture for thousands of years.* || *She is a person of culture and refinement.* **3** [C] (in medicine) a small piece of material from the body tested for a disease: *The doctor took a culture from my sore throat to see if I have a strep throat.*

In recent years, anthropologists have begun to study the role of grandmothers. Anthropologists are scientists who study people, societies, and **cultures.**

   a. Anthropologists study small pieces of material from a body to test it for a disease.

   b. Anthropologists study the achievements of a people or nation in art, music, literature, etc.

   c. Anthropologists study the ideas, activities (art, foods, businesses), and ways of behaving that are special to a country, people, or region.

2 | **role** *n.* **1** a part played by an actor or actress: *She plays the leading role in a television show.* **2** a part or job one takes in a group: *When he married, he had to get used to the role of husband.*

Many biologists and anthropologists now believe that the **role** of grandmothers in a family is very important.

   a. Many biologists and anthropologists now believe that the part played by an actor or actress as grandmothers in a family is very important.

   b. Many biologists and anthropologists now believe that the job a grandmother takes in the family group is very important.

3 chance *n.* **1** [U] the way some things happen for no obvious reason, by accident, etc., luck: *When she arrived late for her train, chance was on her side; the train was running late and had not yet left.* **2** [C; U] the possibility of s.t. happening, probability: *There is a good chance that it will snow tomorrow.* **3** [C] an opportunity: *I had the chance to go to San Francisco on vacation.* **4** **as chance would have it**: luck was (or) was not helping me: *As chance would have it, my old girlfriend and my new girlfriend live in the same apartment building.* **5** **by chance**: accidentally: *We met by chance at the library.* **6** [U] **games of chance**: games of luck: *Some people like to play games of chance, such as cards, dice, and slot machines.* **7** **on the (off) chance that**: on the possibility that: *On the chance that he was going to the store, I asked him to buy toothpaste.* **8** [C] **to take a chance**: to take a risk: *She took a chance by crossing the busy street against the traffic light, but was not hurt.*

In many cultures, having a grandmother in the family made a significant difference in a child's **chances** of living.

a. In many cultures, having a grandmother made a significant difference in a child's probability of living.

b. In many cultures, having a grandmother made a significant difference in a child's happening for no obvious reason.

c. In many cultures, having a grandmother made a significant difference in a child's opportunity of living.

Ⓕ Word Forms

In English, some verbs become nouns by adding the suffix *-tion*—for example, *collect (v.), collection (n.).* Complete each sentence with the correct form of the words on the left. **Use the correct tense of the verb in either the affirmative or the negative form.**

inform *(v.)*

information *(n.)*

① We needed some _____ about the train schedule from New York to Boston. We went to the ticket window, and the clerk _____ us that trains leave for Boston every hour.

populate (v.)

population (n.)

(2) Native Americans first _____ the Western Hemisphere many thousands of years ago. They came in many groups. These first Americans spread all over North and South America, and their _____ grew.

examine (v.)

examination (n.)

(3) Yolanda is having problems with her car. Tomorrow her mechanic _____ it to see what's wrong. Yolanda's mechanic uses a computer to help with his _____ of the problems.

explain (v.)

explanation (n.)

(4) John's three-year-old son asked, "Why is the sky blue?" John had no simple _____ to give him. John _____ why the sky is blue. He said, "Ask your mother."

reduce (v.)

reduction (n.)

(5) Daniel went shopping during a sale. The store _____ the price of a coat he wanted to buy. The price _____ was 50 percent! Daniel was very happy.

PART 2

In English, some adjectives change to nouns by dropping the final -t and adding -ce—for example, *dependent (adj.), dependence (n.)*. Complete each sentence with a correct form of the words on the left. **Use the singular or plural form of the noun.**

important (adj.)

importance (n.)

(1) Yesterday, the college made an _____ announcement about new exams. All the students understood the _____ of this announcement.

different (adj.)

difference (n.)

2 Although Maria and Sarah are twins, they look _____. They are not identical twins. There are a few _____ in their appearance. Maria is taller than Sarah and has blue eyes and blonde hair. Sarah has brown eyes and brown hair.

absent (adj.)

absence (n.)

3 It snowed very hard last night. As a result, many students were _____ from school. Because of the number of _____, the teacher cancelled the class.

present (adj.)

presence (n.)

4 The entire family's _____ was requested at Catherine's wedding. Catherine was very happy to have all of her relatives _____ on her wedding day.

significant (adj.)

significance (n.)

5 Cell phones have had a very _____ effect on people's lives. Today, people can make telephone calls anywhere. The _____ of this technology and its effect on our everyday lives has been surprising.

Word Partnership	Use *significance* with:
adj.	**cultural** significance, **great** significance, **historic** significance, **political** significance, **religious** significance
v.	**downplay the** significance **of** *something*, **explain the** significance **of** *something*, **understand the** significance **of** *something*

G Vocabulary in Context

absent *(adj.)*	mortality *(n.)*	survive *(v.)*
factor *(n.)*	present *(adj.)*	treat *(n.)*
household *(n.)*	reduce *(v.)*	
influence *(v.)*	significant *(adj.)*	

Read the sentences below. Complete each blank space with the correct word from the list above. Use each word only once.

1 Our teacher enjoys holidays. The day before a holiday, she brings in a _____ for every student, and we read about the holiday.

2 The law requires people to wear seat belts in cars. This law has helped to _____ the number of injuries and deaths from car accidents.

3 The _____ rate from car accidents has also decreased as a result of other improvements to cars, such as better brakes.

4 Every 10 years, the U.S. government counts the number of people who live in the United States. The government gets information, such as family income, from every _____ in the country.

5 An important _____ that helps children survive is the availability of clean water and healthy food.

6 Jane moved to another state last year. One of the most _____ changes in her life was adapting to the difference in weather. Florida is very different from Maine!

7 Our friends often _____ the decisions we make, for example, the type of clothes we wear.

8 Susan was _____ from class yesterday, so she called Ana to ask about the homework.

9 The Mayor had a serious announcement to make, so all the reporters from the city's newspapers were _____ at the Mayor's meeting.

10 When their house caught fire, the family was able to _____ by climbing out of a window on the second floor and jumping to the ground. No one was seriously hurt.

H Critical Thinking Strategies

Read the following questions and think about the answers. Write your answer below each question. Then compare your answers with those of your classmates.

1 Children who lived with their grandmother had a higher survival rate than children who didn't live with their grandmothers. What do you think are some reasons for this?

_____

_____

_____

_____

_____

2 Children whose maternal grandmothers lived with them had a higher rate of survival than children whose paternal grandmothers lived with them. Why do you think there was such a significant difference?

_____

_____

_____

_____

_____

I Topics for Discussion and Writing

1 In your culture, do grandparents often live with a married child? If so, do they live with a son or a daughter? Think about how grandmothers interact with their sons' children and with their daughters' children. Do they treat the children the same or differently? Explain your answer.

2 In different cultures, the survival rate of children differs, depending on whether the maternal grandmother is present. Children's survival rate does not improve when the paternal grandmother is present. What may be some explanations for this difference? In other words, what do paternal grandmothers and maternal grandmothers do that is different?

3 In our modern world, is it still important for grandparents to live in the same household with their grandchildren? Explain your reasons for your answer.

4 **Write in your journal.** Imagine that you have married children and that they have children. Will you treat your sons' children and your daughters' children the same? Why or why not?

Follow-Up Activities

1 Dr. Harald A. Euler is a professor of psychology at the University of Kassell in Germany. He interviewed people about their grandparents. Seven hundred people said that all four of their grandparents were alive until they, the grandchildren, were at least seven years old. Examine the pie chart below. Complete the sentences that follow.

Favorite Grandparent

All other responses
36%

Maternal grandmother
50%

Paternal grandmother
14%

a. Among the Germans who were interviewed, their favorite grandparent was their _____

b. Their second favorite was their _____

c. Thirty-six percent of the Germans gave different responses. What do you think the other responses were? Read the list below and check the responses you think different people gave.

_____ My paternal grandfather was my favorite grandparent.

_____ My maternal grandfather was my favorite grandparent.

_____ All of my grandparents died when I was a baby.

_____ I liked all of my grandparents the same. I do not have a favorite.

_____ My grandparents liked me the best of all their grandchildren.

_____ I did not like any of my grandparents.

2 Dr. Donna Leonetti and Dr. Dilip C. Nath are anthropologists at the University of Washington. They studied two groups of people who live in northeast India today. These groups are Bengali and Khasi, and they have some cultural similarities. For example, the Bengali and the Khasi both have low incomes and do heavy manual labor.

There is one big difference between these cultures. When Bengali couples marry, they live with the husband's parents. When Khasi couples marry, they live with the wife's parents. As a result, Bengali children grow up with their paternal grandparents, and Khasi children grow up with their maternal grandparents.

Examine the bar graph below. Answer the questions that follow.

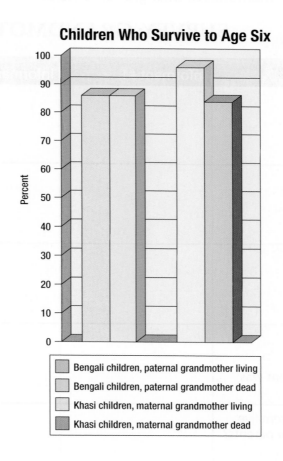

Children Who Survive to Age Six

- Bengali children, paternal grandmother living
- Bengali children, paternal grandmother dead
- Khasi children, maternal grandmother living
- Khasi children, maternal grandmother dead

a. For the Bengali children, did it make a difference in their survival rate to have their paternal grandmother living? _____ Yes _____ No

b. For the Khasi children, did it make a difference in their survival rate to have their maternal grandmother living? _____ Yes _____ No

c. What conclusion can we make from the information about the Bengali and Khasi grandmothers?

1. Paternal grandmothers and maternal grandmothers treat their grandchildren the same.
2. Paternal grandmothers and maternal grandmothers treat their grandchildren differently.

3 Refer to the questionnaire below. Go out alone or in pairs. Survey two or three people. Then bring back your data and combine it with the other students' information. How do these results compare with the answers you discussed in your class? Can you make any general statements about the results of your survey? Do people from the same country have similar memories of their grandmothers?

SURVEY: GRANDMOTHERS

	Informant #1	Informant #2	Informant #3
Gender			
Nationality			
Age			
Think about your grandparents. 1. Which grandparent was your favorite?			
2. Did this grandparent live with you and your parents?			
3. Why was this grandparent your favorite?			

Cloze Quiz

Read the passage below. Fill in the blanks with one word from the list. Use each word only once.

absence	factors	memories	role
anthropologists	grandmothers	mortality	significant
childhood	household	population	survival
discovery	influence	presence	treats
examine	maternal	reduced	whether

What do you think of when you think about your grandmothers? Many people have happy _____ of their grandmothers. Their grandmothers loved them, paid attention to them, and gave them special _____, such as toys and sweets. It seems that for many people, their grandmothers were a very happy part of their _____.
(1)
(2)
(3)

In recent years, anthropologists have begun to study the role of grandmothers. _____ are scientists who study people, societies, and cultures. They studied infants and children to learn about the _____ that helped infants and children survive. Now they are studying how grandmothers _____ the survival rate of their grandchildren.
(4)
(5)
(6)

Biologists and anthropologists are starting to _____ grandmothers within different societies and cultures. In fact, at one international conference, the _____ of grandmothers was the main topic. Some people at the conference studied different societies. They explained that in many cultures, having a grandmother in the family made a _____ difference in the child's chances of living. In fact, the grandmother's presence sometimes improved a child's chance of _____ even more than the father's _____ did. In other words, it was sometimes more important for a child to have a grandmother than for a child to have a father!
(7)
(8)
(9)
(10)
(11)

Dr. Ruth Mace and Dr. Rebecca Sear collected and studied information about people in Gambia, Africa. They discovered that the presence or _____ of the child's father did not affect the death rate. However, the presence of a grandmother _____ the children's chances of dying by 50%. The children were only helped by the presence of their _____ grandmother—their mother's mother. The presence of their father's mother, or paternal grandmother, had no effect on the _____ rate.

Dr. Cheryl Jamison is an anthropologist at Indiana University in Bloomington. She studied the _____ records of a village in central Japan for the period 1671 through 1871. They studied girl and boy children separately and looked for the presence of _____. Again, the anthropologists were surprised by their _____. The death rate for girls was not different _____ or not a grandmother lived with them. However, there was a great difference in the survival rate of boys. If a maternal grandmother lived in the _____, boys were 52% less likely to die in childhood.

Crossword Puzzle

Read the clues on the next page. Write the answers in the correct spaces in the puzzle.

Crossword Puzzle Clues

2. The _____ rate refers to the death rate.
5. Ability
8. Susan is unique. She is _____ anyone I have ever met.
9. John is very _____. He has many friends.
10. My father's parents are my _____ grandparents.
11. The past tense of **do**
13. Habitual
15. Very young children _____ before they can make real words.
16. **He**, _____, **it**
17. Not permanent; only for a time
18. Different
22. An _____ is a person who studies people, cultures, and societies.
23. I live in _____ United States.

1. Sophisticated; not simple
3. A _____ is a person who studies languages.
4. Mary watched her baby carefully to make an _____ about his development.
6. Affect
7. Inborn
9. Some children call their father Daddy; other children call their father _____.
12. Apples are my _____ fruit. I like apples better than any other fruit.
14. My mother's parents are my _____ grandparents.
16. Some people are able to _____ under very difficult conditions.
19. He has; I _____
20. As children _____ up, their language develops.
21. Man, woman, _____, girl

1. The three topics in this unit discuss different issues in society. How do you think language skills, loneliness, and the role of grandmothers are related? How do they affect each other?

    _____

    _____

    _____

2. Many children live in an extended family. That is, they live with their parents and with grandparents, and perhaps other relatives, too. Do you think their language development is influenced by the presence of more adults? Explain your reasons for your answers.

    _____

    _____

    _____

3. Do people who live in extended families experience less loneliness than people who live in a nuclear family, i.e., a family with parents and children? Explain your reasons for your answers.

    _____

    _____

    _____

Justice and Crime

7
CHAPTER

Innocent until Proven Guilty: The Criminal Court System

Prereading Preparation

1. In groups of three or four, discuss the job of the police. What do you think their responsibilities should be? What should they have the authority to do?

2. Read the title of this chapter. In the American legal system, a person accused of a crime is considered to be innocent until he or she is proven guilty in a court. In your country, does an accused person have to prove his or her innocence, or does the court have to prove the person's guilt?

3. Refer to the photo on page 117. The woman represents justice. Why is she blindfolded? What do the scales in her right hand symbolize? What does the sword in her left hand symbolize?

Innocent until Proven Guilty: The Criminal Court System

1   The purpose of the American court system is to protect the rights of the
2   people. According to American law, if someone is accused of a crime, he or she
3   is considered innocent until the court proves that the person is guilty. In other
4   words, it is the responsibility of the court to prove that a person is guilty. It is
5   not the responsibility of the person to prove that he or she is innocent.

6   In order to arrest a person, the police have to be reasonably sure that a crime
7   has been committed. The police must give the suspect the reasons why they are
8   arresting him and tell him his rights under the law.[1] Then the police take the
9   suspect to the police station to "book" him. "Booking" means that the name of
10 the person and the charges against him are formally listed at the police station.

11 The next step is for the suspect to go before a judge. The judge decides
12 whether the suspect should be kept in jail or released. If the suspect has no
13 previous criminal record and the judge feels that he will return to court rather
14 than run away—for example, because he owns a house and has a family—he can
15 go free. Otherwise, the suspect must put up bail.[2] At this time, too, the judge will
16 appoint a court lawyer to defend the suspect if he can't afford one.

17 The suspect returns to court a week or two later. A lawyer from the district
18 attorney's office presents a case against the suspect. This is called a hearing. The
19 attorney may present evidence as well as witnesses. The judge at the hearing
20 then decides whether there is enough reason to hold a trial. If the judge decides
21 that there is sufficient evidence to call for a trial, he or she sets a date for the
22 suspect to appear in court to formally plead guilty or not guilty.

23 At the trial, a jury of 12 people listens to the evidence from both attorneys
24 and hears the testimony of the witnesses. Then the jury goes into a private
25 room to consider the evidence and decide whether the defendant is guilty of the
26 crime. If the jury decides that the defendant is innocent, he goes free. However,
27 if he is convicted, the judge sets a date for the defendant to appear in court
28 again for sentencing. At this time, the judge tells the convicted person what his
29 punishment will be. The judge may sentence him to prison, order him to pay a
30 fine, or place him on probation.[3]

[1] The police must say, "You have the right to remain silent. Anything you say can and will be used against you in a court of law. You have the right to speak to a lawyer and to have the lawyer present during questioning. If you so desire, and cannot afford one, a lawyer will be appointed without any charge before any questioning. Do you understand these rights as I have explained them to you?" These rights are called the Miranda rights.

[2] Bail is an amount of money that the accused person pays to the court to assure that he will return to the court on the trial date. If the person comes back, the money is returned to him. If not, the court keeps the bail money.

[3] Probation means that the convicted person does not have to go to jail. Instead, he must follow certain rules and he is supervised by a parole officer.

31   The American justice system is very complex and sometimes operates slowly.
32   However, every step is designed to protect the rights of the people. These
33   individual rights are the basis, or foundation, of the American government.

Fact-Finding Exercise

Read the passage again. Read the following statements. Check whether they
are True or False. If a statement is false, rewrite the statement so that it is true.
Then go back to the passage and find the line that supports your answer.

1 _____ True _____ False   According to American law, the court must
                                prove that a suspect is innocent.

_____

2 _____ True _____ False   The police decide if a suspect stays in jail or can
                                be released.

_____

3 _____ True _____ False   The judge appoints a court lawyer for a suspect
                                who cannot pay for one.

_____

4 _____ True _____ False An attorney can present evidence or witnesses at the hearing.

_____

5 _____ True _____ False There are 12 people on a jury.

_____

6 _____ True _____ False At a trial, the judge decides if the suspect is guilty or innocent.

_____

7 _____ True _____ False The jury gives the convicted person his punishment after the trial.

_____

B # Reading Analysis

Read each question carefully. Circle the letter or the number of the correct answer, or write your answer in the space provided.

1 What is the main idea of the passage?
  a. According to the American court system, a suspect must prove that she or he is innocent.
  b. The American court system is very complex and was designed to protect the rights of the people.
  c. According to the American court system, a judge decides if a suspect is innocent or guilty.

2 Read lines 2 and 3: " . . . he or she is considered innocent . . . ." This means
  a. the law assumes the suspect is innocent
  b. the law must prove the suspect is innocent

3 Read lines 3 and 4. What follows **in other words?**
  a. An example of the previous sentence
  b. A restatement of the previous sentence
  c. A new idea about the court system

4 Read lines 6 and 7. **Reasonably sure** means

    a. very sure

    b. not sure

    c. a little sure

5 Read lines 7 and 8: "The police . . . tell him his rights under the law."

    a. What are these rights called?

    _____

    b. How do you know?

    _____

    c. This information is called a

        1. direction

        2. footnote

        3. preface

6 Read lines 8–10.

    a. In line 9, what does **"booking"** mean?

    _____

    b. Why does this word have quotation marks (" ") around it?

        1. It is a new word.

        2. Someone is saying this word in the reading.

        3. It is a special meaning of the word _book_ that the police use.

7 Read lines 12–15.

    a. **He can go free** means

        1. the suspect is not guilty

        2. the suspect does not have to go to trial because the judge has decided he is innocent

        3. the suspect does not have to wait in jail or pay money until he goes to trial

    b. **Otherwise** means

        1. if not

        2. in addition

        3. in contrast

    c. Read the footnote describing **bail.** What is the purpose of having the suspect pay bail?

        1. To pay for the judge and the trial

        2. As insurance that the suspect will return to court

        3. To pay for a court lawyer to defend the suspect

8 Read lines 17 and 18. What is a **hearing?**

_____

_____

9 Read lines 19–22. What is a synonym for **enough reason?**

_____

10 In line 26, **however** means
   a. also
   b. next
   c. but

11 Read lines 26–30.
   a. What is **sentencing?**
      1. Subjects, verbs, and objects
      2. The date the defendant must appear in court
      3. The punishment that the judge gives the defendant

   b. Read the footnote about **probation**. What is the purpose of probation?
      1. To make sure the convicted person behaves well
      2. To save the court some money

12 **a.** Read lines 32 and 33. What is a synonym for **basis?**

_____

   b. How do you know?

_____

C

Information Organization

Read the passage again. Underline what you think are the main ideas. Then scan the reading and complete the following flowchart, using the sentences that you have underlined to help you. You will use this flowchart later to answer questions about the reading.

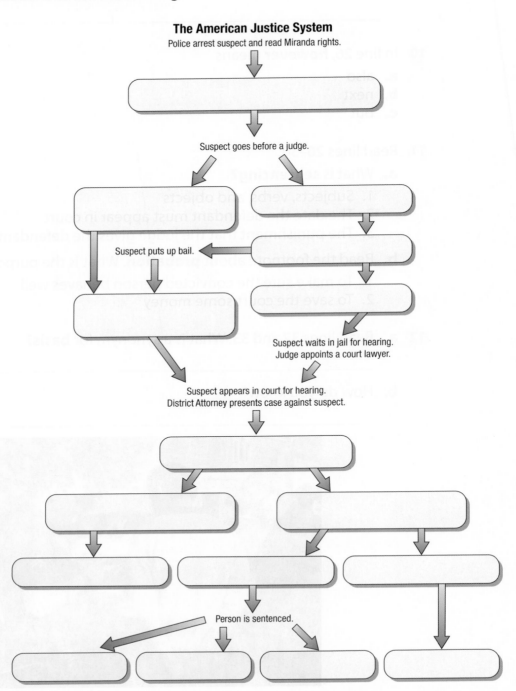

The American Justice System

Police arrest suspect and read Miranda rights.

Suspect goes before a judge.

Suspect puts up bail.

Suspect waits in jail for hearing.
Judge appoints a court lawyer.

Suspect appears in court for hearing.
District Attorney presents case against suspect.

Person is sentenced.

D Information Recall and Summary

Read each question carefully. Use your flowchart to answer the questions. Do not refer back to the passage. When you are finished, write a brief summary of the reading.

1 What must the police do after they arrest a suspect?

_____

_____

2 What happens to the suspect after the police book him or her?

_____

_____

_____

_____

_____

3 What happens at a trial? Describe it.

_____

_____

_____

4 If a person is proven innocent, what happens?

_____

5 If a person is convicted, what happens?

_____

Summary

Work in pairs or alone. Write a brief summary of the reading, and put it on the board. Compare your summary with your classmates'. Which one best describes the main idea of the reading?

_____

_____

_____

Dictionary Skills

Read the following sentences. Use the context to help you understand the boldface words. Read the dictionary entry for that word and circle the appropriate definition. Then rewrite the sentence, using the definition you have chosen. Be sure to make your sentence grammatically correct.

1

> **charge** *n.* **1** [C] price: *What is the charge for a night in that hotel?* **2** [C] a purchase made on credit: *Will you pay cash or will this be a charge?* **3** [C] a fast move forward, surge: *The soldiers made a charge up the hill.* **4** [C; U] **a.** an ability in some substances to cause electrical events: *There are two types of electrical charges, negative and positive.* **b.** a measure of the amount of this ability in s.t.: *The charge in my car battery is low.* **5** [C] a statement of blame against s.o.: *a charge against s.o. in a court of law* || *The charge of drunk driving, if one is found guilty, carries a large fine.* **6** [C] s.o. put in another's care: *The baby-sitter took her two young charges to the park.* **7** [C] *frml.* a responsibility, mission: *As sales manager, my charge is to hire 20 new sales representatives.* **8** *sing.infrml.* excitement: *She gets a charge out of cliff diving.* **9 to be in charge (of):** to be in control or command (of): *I'm leaving you in charge while I'm gone.* || *She's in charge of the new project.*

The police list the **charges** against a suspect in a book at the police station.

_____

2

> **record** *n.* **1** s.t. (usu. written) that proves that an event happened, including records of business transactions, scientific data, cultural, or other human activities: *The records of our business are kept in our computer and in printouts.* **2** the best time, distance, etc., in an athletic event: *She holds the world record for the 100-meter dash.* **3** a criminal's history of arrests and things he or she did wrong: *That thief has a long criminal record.* **4** a flat, black disk onto which a sound recording, esp. music, has been pressed: *He has a collection of Elvis Presley records from the 1950s.* **5 to break the record:** to make a new fastest time, distance, etc.: *A runner broke the world record for the 100-meter run yesterday.* **6 for the record:** indicating s.t. official for the public or for clarity: *The lawyer told the court, for the record, that the woman he represented would not officially speak in court.* **7 off the record:** referring to s.t. that should not be heard by the public, (*syn.*) unofficial: *The mayor called in reporters to talk to them off the record about the latest crime wave, and asked them not to publish what he said in their newspapers.* **8 on the record:** referring to s.t. that can be made public, (*syn.*) official: *The mayor then spoke on the record about what his plans are for fighting crime.*

The police may not have any **record** of criminal activity for a particular suspect.

_____

3 **step** *n.* **1** a walking movement, the act of lifting the foot, moving it forward, and putting it down: *The baby took her first step today!* **2** the distance of this movement: *The shopping area is a few steps from the parking lot.* **3** one surface in a set of stairs: *She came partway downstairs, stopping on the bottom step.* **4** *n.pl.* **steps**: a set of stairs, staircase: *We put flowerpots on the front steps of the house.* **5** one action toward a goal: *the first step in our plan* **6** (in music) one tone up or down in a scale **7** **in step with** or **out of step with**: **a.** moving at the same (or) different pace or rhythm as others: *The soldier was in step with the others in the parade.* **b.** *fig.* understanding and doing (or) not understanding and not doing as others do: *My grandmother is out of step with today's music.* **8** **to keep step with**: **a.** to march or walk in exactly the same way as others: *The little boy kept step with his mother, although her legs were longer.* **b.** *fig.* to stay aware of what's going on: *He keeps step with the computer business by reading lots of magazines.* **9** **step by step**: one section or part at a time: *She learned how to change a tire step by step.* **10** **step up**: a higher or better position: *Moving from secretary to salesman was a step up for him.* **11** **step-up**: an increase: *a step-up in factory production since last year* **12** **to take steps**: to take necessary actions in order to get s.t. done: *The hospital is taking steps to give better care by hiring more nurses.* **13** **to watch one's step**: **a.** to be careful walking: *Watch your step; there's a bump in the sidewalk.* **b.** *fig.* to be careful: *Tell the girl to watch her step with matches or she'll start a fire.*

The judge's first **step** is to decide whether to keep the suspect in jail or to allow him to go free until the hearing.

---

4 **present** *v.* [T] **1** to offer, put forth for consideration: *She presented her idea for a new product at the last sales meeting.* **2** to give: *The mayor presented him with an award for good citizenship.* || *The doctor presented his bill.* **3** to bring to meet s.o., esp. of greater importance: *The ambassador was presented to the Queen at court.* **4** to cause or represent: *The snow was so deep that it presented a problem to people trying to walk.* **5** to perform: *to present a play*

The district attorney's office **presents** evidence against a suspect.

> **5**   **consider**   *v.* **1** [I; T] to think about s.t.: *I will consider your offer and tell you my decision tomorrow.* **2** [T] to debate: *Congress considered the new tax and voted it down.* **3** [T] to have an opinion about s.t.: *He considers this to be the best book on the subject.* **4** **all things considered**: in view of everything: *All things considered, our old car is no good, so we should buy a new one now.* See: considering.

The jury goes into a private room in order to **consider** the evidence against the suspect and decide whether the suspect is innocent or guilty.

_____

_____

F   Word Forms

PART 1

In English, some adjectives become nouns by adding the suffix *-ity*—for example, *national (adj.)* becomes *nationality (n.)*. Complete each sentence with the correct form of the words on the left. **Use the singular or the plural form of the noun.**

responsible *(adj.)*

responsibility *(n.)*

(1) Employees have many _____ to their employers. Employees are usually _____ for coming to work on time, for being productive at work, and for being honest with their employer.

formal *(adj.)*

formality *(n.)*

(2) On very _____ occasions, Americans like to dress up, especially when they go out. However, at home, Americans do not observe the same _____. For example, men usually do not wear a suit when they eat dinner at home.

complex (*adj.*)
complexity (*n.*)

(3) Today, a car is quite a _____ machine. New cars have computers and advanced sound systems. In the past, however, cars were much simpler. _____ in machinery developed over many years as technology advanced.

individual (*adj.*)
individuality (*n.*)

(4) In general, people value their _____. Even when they are part of a group, people enjoy making _____ decisions.

public (*adj.*)
publicity (*n.*)

(5) The mayor made a very unpopular _____ announcement yesterday. He received considerable negative _____ when he announced that he planned to reduce many city services.

PART 2

In English, verbs become nouns in several ways. Some verbs become nouns by adding the suffix -ment—for example, *govern* (*v.*) becomes *government* (*n.*). Complete each sentence with the correct form of the words on the left. **Use the correct tense of the verb in either the affirmative or the negative form. Use the singular or plural form of the noun.**

appoint (*v.*)
appointment (*n.*)

(1) In a few weeks, the President _____ a new ambassador to Japan. This is a very important _____ because Japan is an economically powerful country.

punish (*v.*)
punishment (*n.*)

(2) In the American court system, a judge tries to make the _____ fit the crime. For instance, a judge _____ a convicted person with life in prison for stealing a bicycle.

judge (v.)

judgment (n.)

3 A person who _____ a trial must be impartial when making decisions. In a court of law, _____ must be made fairly and objectively.

disagree (v.)

disagreement (n.)

4 Allison and Clark had several _____ about redecorating their home. In fact, they _____ on almost everything: paint color, furniture, carpets, and lights.

establish (v.)

establishment (n.)

5 In the United States, the permanent _____ of a democratic government took several years. The United States _____ a constitutional government in 1787.

Word Partnership	Use *establish* with:
n.	establish **control**, establish **independence**, establish **rules,** establish **contact**, establish **relations,** establish *someone's* **identity**

G

Vocabulary in Context

appoint (v.)	**establish** (v.)	**purpose** (n.)
basis (n.)	**however** (adv.)	**record** (n.)
case (n.)	**otherwise** (adv.)	
consider (v.)	**present** (v.)	

Read the following sentences. Complete each blank space with the correct word or phrase from the list above. Use each word only once.

1. The Board of Health keeps an accurate _____ of all births and deaths in the city.

2. Holly worked very hard before she was able to _____ her own business, but eventually, she was successful.

3. If it snows this week, we will go skiing this weekend. _____ we will stay in the city and see a movie.

4. The students always _____ a class representative for the student council at the beginning of the semester.

5. Every fall, television stations _____ new programs to their viewers.

6. When deciding on a college, you need to _____ several factors, including the cost of tuition, the courses offered, and the location of the college.

7. The ability to read and write well is the _____ of a good education.

8. I don't understand the _____ of this machine. What is it used for?

9. I prefer to eat only fresh vegetables. _____, when they are not available, I eat frozen or canned vegetables.

10. Have you read about the killing in the library last year? The police have been trying to solve that murder _____ for months, but so far they haven't been successful.

H Critical Thinking Strategies

Read the following questions and think about the answers. Write your answer below each question. Then compare your answers with those of your classmates.

1. The jury goes into a private room to decide if a suspect is guilty or innocent. No one can come into the room except the jury. What do you think is the reason for this?

   _____

   _____

2. In the United States, a person cannot be tried twice for the same crime. For example, if a person is accused of murder, but a jury acquits him, and later it is discovered that the person really did commit the murder, the person stays free.

   a. Why do you think this is part of the American justice system? Why do you think this custom exists?

   _____

   _____

   _____

   b. Do you think this is fair and just? Explain your reasons.

   _____

   _____

   _____

I Topics for Discussion and Writing

1. Work in small groups. The government has asked you to review the present procedure for arresting and booking a suspect. Review the steps involved in arresting and charging a person with a crime. Discuss what you would and would not change. Present your revised procedure to the class.

2 In the United States, trials are not held in secret. The public may sit in the courtroom and observe the proceedings. Visit a courtroom with two or three of your classmates. Observe what takes place. Report back to the class.

3 **Write in your journal.** Would you want to be part of a jury? Why or why not?

Follow-Up Activities

1 Refer to the chart in Exercise C, which lists the American procedure for arresting and trying a person for a crime. Compare this system with the system in your country. Using the following chart, compare the two systems, and write what you see as the advantages and disadvantages of each.

	In the United States	In _____
Procedure	Police arrest the suspect and read Miranda rights.	
Advantage		
Disadvantage		
Procedure		
Advantage		
Disadvantage		
Procedure		
Advantage		
Disadvantage		

2 Read about a criminal case in the news. Bring several newspaper and magazine articles on the case into class. In groups, form juries. Read through the evidence and decide whether the suspect is guilty or innocent. If your group decides the suspect is guilty, appoint a judge from your group to decide on a sentence.

K Cloze Quiz

Read the passage below. Fill in the blanks with one word from the list. Use each word only once.

appear	evidence	innocent	prove	time
consider	guilty	jury	punishment	whether
crime	hears	people	purpose	witnesses
defendant	however	protect	responsibility	words

The _____ of the American court system is to _____ the
(1)   (2)
rights of the _____. According to American law, if someone is accused
(3)
of a _____, he is considered _____ until the court proves that
(4)   (5)
the person is guilty. In other _____, it is the responsibility of the court
(6)
to _____ that a person is _____. It is not the _____ of
(7)   (8)   (9)
the person to prove that he is innocent.

At a trial, a jury of 12 men and women listens to the _____ from
(10)
both attorneys and _____ the testimony of the _____. Then
(11)   (12)
the _____ goes into a private room to _____ the evidence
(13)   (14)
and decide _____ the defendant is guilty of the crime. If the jury
(15)
decides that the _____ is innocent, he goes free. _____, if he
(16)   (17)
is convicted, the judge sets a date for the defendant to _____ in court
(18)
again for sentencing. At this _____, the judge tells the convicted
(19)
person what his _____ will be.
(20)

UNIT 3 JUSTICE AND CRIME

8
CHAPTER

The Reliability of Eyewitnesses

Prereading Preparation

1 Look at the photograph. Where was this photograph taken? Who are the four women? Why are they there?

_____

_____

2 What kinds of evidence are used to convict suspected criminals? In small groups, use the chart below to make a list of the kinds of evidence used to convict criminals for the crimes listed.

Crime	Murder	Bank Robbery	Mugging
Types			
of			
Evidence			

3   In your country, what kinds of evidence are used to convict criminals for these crimes?

_____

_____

4   In your country, is an eyewitness's testimony important in convicting criminals?

_____

5   In your opinion, what kinds of people make reliable eyewitnesses? Why?

_____

_____

Track 8

The Reliability of Eyewitnesses

1   Bernard Jackson is a free man today, but he has many bitter memories.
2 Jackson spent five years in prison after a jury wrongly convicted him of
3 raping two women. At Jackson's trial, although two witnesses testified that
4 Jackson was with them in another location at the times of the crimes, he was
5 convicted anyway. Why? The jury believed the testimony of the two victims,
6 who positively identified Jackson as the man who had attacked them. The
7 court eventually freed Jackson after the police found the man who had really
8 committed the crimes. Jackson was similar in appearance to the guilty man.
9 The two women had made a mistake in identity. As a result, Jackson has lost
10 five years of his life.
11   The two women in this case were eyewitnesses. They clearly saw the man
12 who attacked them, yet they mistakenly identified an innocent person. Similar
13 incidents have occurred before. Eyewitnesses to other crimes have identified the
14 wrong person in a police lineup or in photographs.

15 Many factors influence the accuracy of eyewitness testimony. For instance,
16 witnesses sometimes see photographs of several suspects before they try to
17 identify the person they saw in a lineup of people. They can become confused by
18 seeing many photographs of similar faces. The number of people in the lineup,
19 and whether it is a live lineup or a photograph, may also affect a witness's
20 decision. People sometimes have difficulty identifying people of other races. The
21 questions the police ask witnesses also have an effect on them.

22 Are some witnesses more reliable than others? Many people believe that
23 police officers are more reliable than ordinary people. Psychologists decided to
24 test this idea, and they discovered that it is not true. Two psychologists showed
25 a film of crimes to both police officers and civilians. The psychologists found
26 no difference between the police and the civilians in correctly remembering the
27 details of the crimes.

28 Despite all the possibilities for inaccuracy, courts cannot exclude eyewitness
29 testimony from a trial. American courts depend almost completely on
30 eyewitness testimony to resolve court cases. Sometimes it is the only evidence
31 to a crime, such as rape. Furthermore, eyewitness testimony is often correct.
32 Although people do sometimes make mistakes, many times they really do
33 identify individuals correctly.

34 American courts depend on the ability of the 12 jurors, and not the judges,
35 to determine the accuracy of the witness's testimony. It is their responsibility to
36 decide if a certain witness could actually see, hear, and remember what occurred.

37 In a few cases, the testimony of eyewitnesses has convicted innocent people.
38 More importantly, it has rightly convicted a larger number of guilty people;
39 consequently, it continues to be of great value in the American judicial system.

Fact-Finding Exercise

Read the passage again. Read the following statements. Check whether they are True or False. If a statement is false, rewrite the statement so that it is true. Then go back to the passage and find the line that supports your answer.

1 _____ True _____ False   Bernard Jackson went to jail for five years because he was guilty.

_____

2 _____ True _____ False   Bernard Jackson looked like the guilty man, but he was innocent.

_____

3 _____ True _____ False   The eyewitnesses in Jackson's trial were wrong.

_____

4 _____ True _____ False   Some witnesses become confused when they see too many photographs of similar people.

_____

5 _____ True _____ False   Police officers are better witnesses than ordinary people.

_____

6 _____ True _____ False   American courts depend a lot on eyewitness testimony.

_____

7 _____ True _____ False   The judge must decide if a witness's story is accurate.

_____

Reading Analysis

Read each question carefully. Circle the letter or the number of the correct answer, or write your answer in the space provided.

1 What is the main idea of the passage?
  a. Bernard Jackson spent five years in jail, but he was innocent.
  b. Eyewitness testimony, although sometimes incorrect, is valuable.
  c. Police officers are not better eyewitnesses than civilians.

2 According to the passage, which of the following factors influence eyewitnesses? Check the correct ones.

  _____ **a.** Seeing many similar photographs

  _____ **b.** The time of day the crime happened

  _____ **c.** The questions the police ask

  _____ **d.** The age and sex of the witness

  _____ **e.** A live lineup or a photograph of a group of people

  _____ **f.** The type of job the witness has

  _____ **g.** The education of the witness

  _____ **h.** The race of the suspect

3 Read lines 1–3. What are **bitter memories?**
  a. Angry memories
  b. Unhappy memories
  c. Prison memories

4 Read lines 5 and 6.
  a. What does **testimony** mean?
    1. A person's statement used for evidence
    2. A photograph used for evidence
    3. A clue used for evidence

  b. What does **victims** refer to?
    1. The people who commit a crime
    2. The people against whom a crime is committed

5 **a.** In line 12, what does **yet** mean?

    1. After

    2. So

    3. But

    b. How do you know?

_____

_____

6 In line 15, what does **for instance** mean?

    a. In addition

    b. For example

    c. However

7 Read lines 22–24: ". . . they discovered that it is not true."

    a. What is not true? It is not true that

_____

_____

    b. What are **civilians?**

        1. Police officers

        2. Ordinary people

        3. Psychologists

8 Read lines 28–31.

    a. What does **despite** mean?

        1. In addition to

        2. As a result

        3. In spite of

    b. What does **evidence** mean?

        1. Proof

        2. Result

        3. Story

9 Read lines 35 and 36: "It is their responsibility to decide if . . . ." Who does **their** refer to?

    a. The judges

    b. The courts

    c. The jurors

10 Read lines 38 and 39. What does **consequently** mean?

   a. As a result
   b. However
   c. In addition

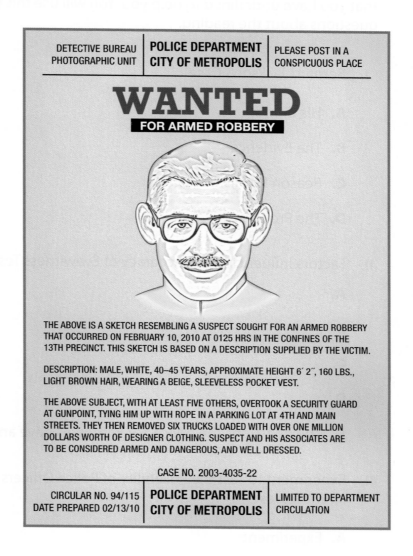

11 Refer to the wanted poster above. In small groups, answer the following questions.

   a. Who is this man?
   b. Who drew this picture?
   c. What do the police think this man did?
   d. Where can you see wanted posters?

Information Organization

Read the passage again. Underline what you think are the main ideas. Then scan the reading and complete the following outline, using the sentences that you have underlined to help you. You will use this outline later to answer questions about the reading.

I. Bernard Jackson's Case

   A. His Crime:

   B. The Evidence:

   C. Reason for His Conviction:

   D. The Problem:

II. Factors Influencing the Accuracy of Eyewitness Testimony

   A.

   B.

   C.

   D.

   E. The questions the police ask witnesses have an effect on them.

III. Experiment to Test the Reliability of Police Officers and Ordinary People as Witnesses

   A. Experiment:

   B. Results:

IV. Why Courts Cannot Exclude Eyewitness Testimony from a Trial

   A.

   B.

Information Recall and Summary

Read each question carefully. Use your outline to answer the questions. Do not refer back to the passage. When you are finished, write a brief summary of the reading.

1 Why did Bernard Jackson go to prison? Was he guilty?

_____

2 At Jackson's trial, what did the two witnesses testify? Did the jury believe the two witnesses?

_____

_____

3 Why did the victims identify Jackson as the man who had attacked them?

_____

4 What are some factors that affect eyewitness testimony?

_____

_____

_____

5 a. Are police officers better witnesses than ordinary people?

_____

b. How did psychologists test this idea?

_____

_____

6 Why is eyewitness testimony important in an American court?

_____

7 In an American court, who decides if the eyewitness testimony is correct or not? Why is eyewitness testimony a valuable part of the American judicial system?

_____

Summary

Work in pairs or alone. Write a brief summary of the reading, and put it on the board. Compare your summary with your classmates'. Which one best describes the main idea of the reading?

_____

_____

_____

_____

_____

E # Dictionary Skills

Read the following sentences. Use the context to help you understand the boldface words. Read the dictionary entry for that word and circle the appropriate definition. Then rewrite the sentence, using the definition you have chosen. Be sure to make your sentence grammatically correct.

1
> **lineup** *n.* **1** (in baseball) a list of players in the order in which they will come to bat: *The starting lineup includes the team's best players.* **2** *fig.* any listing of people, events, products, etc.: *The fall lineup of television programs (new fashions, social events, etc.) looks interesting.* **3** a group of people, including criminal suspects, presented by police to witnesses who try to identify the criminal(s) in the group: *The man who was robbed picked out the thief from the police lineup.*

The number of people in the **lineup**, and whether it is a live lineup or a photograph, may affect a witness's decision.

_____

_____

2 | **exclude** *v.* [T] -cluded, -cluding, -cludes **1** not to include, leave out, (*syn.*) to omit: *I put all but one ingredient into the soup; I excluded the hot peppers.* **2** to keep out, (*syns.*) to prohibit, ban: *The restaurant excludes anyone who is not properly dressed from entering.* -*n.* [U] **exclusion**.

Courts cannot **exclude** eyewitness testimony from a trial. Sometimes it is the only evidence to a crime.

_____

_____

3 | **value** *n.* **1** [U] worth: *Mr. Perez is a rich man who owns many pieces of art of great value.* || *The value of this home has doubled since we bought it.* **2** [U] liking, importance: *She places great value on her friendships with others.* **3** *pl.* ideals, standards of a society: *We have tried to teach our children solid values.*

Eyewitness testimony continues to be of **value** in the American judicial system.

_____

_____

4 | **positive** *adj.* **1** optimistic, hopeful: *He has a positive attitude toward his work; he likes it and does it well.* **2** certain, definite, without doubt: *The police are positive that they have the right man in jail.* **3** indicating yes: *I received a positive reply to my application to enter that college.* **4** helpful, beneficial: *She received positive advice (criticism, insights, etc.) on how to study for exams.* **5** (of the results of a medical test) showing that a condition, disease, etc., exists: *She had a pregnancy test and the result was positive.* **6** indicating a (+) sign for an electrical charge: *I hooked the starter cable to the positive post on the car battery.* -*adv.* **positively.**

The two women were **positive** that Bernard Jackson had committed the crimes against them.

_____

_____

F Word Forms

In English, the verb and noun forms of some words are the same—for example, *change (n.)* and *change (v.)*. Complete each sentence with the correct form of the word on the left. **Use the correct tense of the verb in either the affirmative or the negative form. Use the singular or plural form of the noun. In addition, indicate whether you are using the noun (n.) or verb (v.) form.**

influence

1. Many people believe that the weather _____
(n., v.)
our feelings. However the strength of this

_____ has not been proven.
(n., v.)

film

2. Unfortunately, John _____ our high school reunion
(n., v.)
next month. His _____ of social gatherings are
(n., v.)
always interesting, so we are very disappointed.

attack

3. People frequently write _____ on politicians in
(n., v.)
the newspapers, but the politicians do not always pay

attention to them. People usually _____ the
(n., v.)
politicians' dishonesty.

witness

4. Margaret was the only _____ to a serious car
(n., v.)
accident. As soon as she _____ the accident,
(n., v.)
she called an ambulance and the police.

mistake

5 Susan and Emily are twin sisters. People frequently

_____ Emily for Susan and Susan for
     (n., v.)

Emily because they look alike. Sometimes such

_____ in identity are funny.
     (n., v.)

question

6 The police _____ the suspect until his lawyer
               (n., v.)

arrived. They waited for his lawyer, and then they

asked him very specific _____.
                     (n., v.)

PART 2

In English, there are several ways verbs change to nouns. Some verbs become nouns by adding the suffix *-ence* or *-ance*—for example, *insist (v.)* becomes *insistence (n.)*. Complete each sentence with the correct form of the words on the left. **Use the correct tense of the verb in either the affirmative or the negative form. Use the singular or plural form of the noun.**

depend *(v.)*

dependence *(n.)*

1 When a baby is born, it _____ on its parents completely. As it grows up, the child's _____ on its parents decreases.

differ *(v.)*

difference *(n.)*

2 Angela's coat and Debbie's coat _____ in color. They are both blue. The only _____ between the two coats are their size and material. Angela's coat is cotton, but Debbie's coat is wool.

occur *(v.)*

occurrence *(n.)*

3 Snow in April is an unusual _____ in this area. In fact, snow _____ very often, even in the winter. Only two or three inches fall during the entire season.

assist *(v.)*

assistance *(n.)*

4 The nurses _____ the doctor today, but they will help her during the operation tomorrow. The doctor will need their _____ to give her surgical instruments.

appear *(v.)*

appearance *(n.)*

5 The President made a special _____ on television last night. He _____ very calm, but his news was serious.

Word Partnership	Use *appearance* with:
n.	**court** appearance
adj.	**public** appearance, **sudden** appearance, **physical** appearance
v.	**make an** appearance, **change** *your* appearance

G Vocabulary in Context

bitter *(adj.)*	**guilty** *(adj.)*	**testimony** *(n.)*
civilian *(n.)*	**innocent** *(adj.)*	**victims** *(n.)*
despite *(prep.)*	**mistake** *(n.)*	
evidence *(n.)*	**similar** *(adj.)*	

Read the following sentences. Complete each blank space with the correct word from the list above. Use each word only once.

1 John was in the army for two years. At the end of his military service, he was happy to become a _____ again.

2 Last week, an armed robber shot two men when he robbed the City Bank. Afterwards, an ambulance took the two _____ to the hospital.

3. Tommy stole a car, but the police caught and arrested him. Because Tommy was _____, he went to prison for six months.

4. Kathy saw the two men who robbed City Bank. As a result of her _____ in court, the two men were convicted and put into prison.

5. When the police investigate a crime, they look for _____, such as fingerprints, footprints, hair, and clothing.

6. Mr. Michaels worked for the same company for 25 years. Six months before retiring, he lost his job, and he couldn't find another one. He has become very _____ towards his old company.

7. Many people believed that Ronald had murdered his wife, but he was _____.

8. _____ the cold weather, Kay went to work without her coat.

9. Chris and his brother look very _____. They are both tall and thin, and both have light hair and blue eyes.

10. The waitress made a _____. She gave me coffee, but I had ordered tea.

H Critical Thinking Strategies

Read the following questions and think about the answers. Write your answer below each question. Then compare your answers with those of your classmates.

1. Police officers are not better eyewitnesses than ordinary people. What type of person do you think would be a very reliable eyewitness? Why?

_____

_____

2 Eyewitness testimony is often unreliable. However, it continues to be part of the American legal system. Should eyewitness testimony be eliminated? Why or why not?

_____

_____

I Topics for Discussion and Writing

1 In this article, the two women made a mistake in identity. Think about a case you know of in which an innocent person was convicted of a crime because eyewitnesses made a mistake. Describe the case.

2 Is it possible to be sure of an eyewitness's testimony? Please explain.

3 **Write in your journal.** Have you ever witnessed a crime or an accident? Were you able to remember the exact details? Why or why not? Describe what happened.

J Follow-Up Activities

1 Reread lines 15–21 of the article. What can the police do differently to help avoid cases of mistaken identity? With a partner, read the following sets of questions. Decide which one in each pair is the better question for the police to ask. Compare your choices with your classmates' choices. Be prepared to explain your decisions.

a. _____ 1. What was the suspect wearing?

_____ 2. Was the suspect wearing a shirt and pants, or a suit?

b. _____ 1. Did the suspect have a gun or a knife?

_____ 2. Did the suspect have a weapon? If so, what did you see?

c. _____ 1. Exactly what did the suspect look like? Describe the suspect's face in detail.

_____ 2. Will you look at these photographs and tell us which one is a photo of the suspect?

d. _____ 1. What do you estimate was the suspect's height and weight?

_____ 2. How tall and heavy was the suspect?

2 In this article, the two women made a mistake in identity. There are many factors that can cause people to make an error. Refer to the chart below. Work in small groups with your classmates. Which factors might confuse people and cause them to make mistakes in identity? Why? Write your reasons and rank the factors in the table below. For example, if you think that **weather** is the factor that would confuse people the most, write **1** next to **weather** under **Rank**.

Factor	Reason	Rank
sex (of witness/of suspect)		
race (of witness/of suspect)		
age (of witness/of suspect)		
time of day		
weather		
distance of witness from the crime		
level of education of the witness		

Cloze Quiz

Read the passage below. Fill in the blanks with one word from the list. Use each word only once.

appearance	evidence	instance	reliable
bitter	eyewitness	judges	similar
civilians	guilty	mistake	testimony
crimes	influence	occurred	victims
despite	innocent	questions	yet

Bernard Jackson is a free man today, but he has many _____
(1)
memories. Jackson spent five years in prison after a jury convicted him of
raping two women. Jackson's lawyer introduced witnesses who testified
that Jackson was with them in another location at the times of the crimes.
Why, then, was he convicted? The jury believed the _____ of the
(2)
two _____. They positively identified Jackson as the man who had
(3)
attacked them. The court eventually freed Jackson after the police found
the man who had really committed the crimes. Jackson was similar in
_____ to the guilty man. The two women had made a _____ in
(4)   (5)
identity. As a result, Jackson has lost five years of his life.

The two women in this case were eyewitnesses. They clearly saw the man
who attacked them, _____ they mistakenly identified an innocent
(6)
person. Similar incidents have _____ before. Eyewitnesses to other
(7)
crimes have identified the wrong person in a police lineup or in photographs.

Many factors _____ the accuracy of eyewitness testimony. For
(8)
_____, witnesses sometimes see photographs of several suspects
(9)
before they try to identify the person they saw in a lineup of people. They
can become confused by seeing many photographs of _____ faces.
(10)

UNIT 3 JUSTICE AND CRIME

The number of people in the lineup, and whether it is a live lineup or a photograph, may also affect a witness's decision. People sometimes have difficulty identifying people of other races. The _____ the police ask
(11)
witnesses also have an effect on them.

Are some witnesses more _____ than others? Many people believe
(12)
that police officers are more accurate than ordinary people. Psychologists decided to test this idea, and they discovered that it is not true. Two psychologists showed a film of _____ to both police officers and
(13)
_____. The psychologists found no difference between the two groups
(14)
in correctly remembering the details of the crimes.

_____ all the possibilities for inaccuracy, courts cannot exclude
(15)
eyewitness testimony from a trial. American courts almost completely depend on eyewitness testimony to resolve court cases. Sometimes it is the only _____ to a crime, such as rape. Furthermore, _____ testimony
(16)   (17)
is often correct. Although people do sometimes make mistakes, many times they really do identify individuals correctly.

American courts depend on the ability of the 12 jurors, and not the _____, to determine the accuracy of the witness's testimony. It is
(18)
their responsibility to decide if a certain witness could actually see, hear, and remember what occurred. In a few cases, the testimony of eyewitnesses has convicted _____ people. More importantly, it has rightly convicted
(19)
a larger number of _____ people; consequently, it continues to be a
(20)
valuable part of the American judicial system.

9
CHAPTER

Solving Crimes with Modern Technology

Prereading Preparation

1 Work in a small group. What types of technology can help solve crimes? Make a list in the chart below. When you are finished, share your list with the class.

Type of Technology	How can this help solve a crime?

2 Who are the different people that solve crimes? How are their jobs different from each other's jobs? How do they try to solve crimes?

Solving Crimes with Modern Technology

1   Solving crimes is one of the most important jobs of law enforcement.
2 Improvements in crime technology help detectives solve crimes faster, and
3 more efficiently, today. For example, crime labs have new kinds of DNA testing,
4 which can identify body fluids such as blood, sweat, and saliva. There are also
5 new kinds of fingerprint testing. In the past, fingerprint testing was only helpful
6 if the fingerprints from the crime scene could be matched with "prints" that
7 were already on file. The fingerprints of convicted criminals are kept on file in
8 police records permanently. People whose fingerprints are not on file cannot be
9 identified in this way, and as a result, many crimes have not been solved.

10   However, the newest kind of fingerprint testing can do much more than
11 simply record a fingerprint pattern. It can provide additional information about
12 a fingerprint, such as the age and sex of its owner. The fingerprints can reveal
13 if the person takes medication, too. But the latest technology does even more. It
14 can even get fingerprints from fabric, for example, from blankets or curtains.

15   In a recent case, the police in Tacoma, Washington, found the body of a
16 27-year-old woman who had been murdered in her bedroom. There were no
17 witnesses, and her apartment had few clues. The only real evidence did not
18 seem very helpful. The victim's bed sheet had some of her blood on it and
19 looked as if someone had wiped his or her hands. At the time of the murder, it
20 was impossible to identify a fingerprint, or even a palm print, from fabric. This
21 is because all the unique characteristics of fingerprints and palm prints can get
22 lost in a fabric. The detectives were unable to use the evidence, but they saved it
23 anyway. Then they called Eric Berg, a forensic expert with the Tacoma police, for
24 help. A forensic expert is a person who helps solve crimes.

25   Eric Berg was not only a forensic expert, but a computer expert, too. Using his
26 own time and money, he had already spent years developing computer software
27 in his own home to enhance, or improve, crime scene photos. He decided to use
28 that software to examine the fabric from the murder case. It worked! Eric Berg
29 had used his computer to make the palm print more apparent, or clear. When
30 he was done, he gave the evidence to the detectives. The detectives found a man
31 whose palm print matched a print on file. Only two hours later, the suspect was
32 arrested. He was eventually convicted of the crime and is now in jail. Today,
33 many other police departments use Eric Berg's new software. Because of it,
34 crimes that seemed to be unsolvable were suddenly solvable again.

35   While all of this technology may help solve future crimes, it may also help
36 solve crimes from the past. In all crimes, detectives carefully take samples of
37 evidence from the scene. In many cases 15 or 20 years ago, the police could
38 not always identify important evidence such as body fluids. In these cases,
39 they stored the evidence in a freezer. Now, criminologists have the modern
40 technology they require to examine the frozen evidence, and, in many
41 cases, identify it as well. In Newport News, Virginia, detectives today are
42 reinvestigating a 15-year-old murder case. A 34-year-old woman was murdered,
43 and a pair of scissors was found at the crime scene. The police had only one
44 clue: the scissors. The police found a drop of sweat on the scissors, but they had
45 no way of studying it because, at the time, the DNA technology was not very
46 advanced. Today, however, they are using the new DNA technology and believe
47 it may lead them to the murderer.
48   Today, police have other kinds of new crime-solving technology, as well. A
49 laser system of lights helps detectives find evidence of body fluids at a crime
50 scene in daylight. Previously, it was only possible to see this kind of evidence
51 at night or in the dark. By helping the police identify criminals, this new
52 technology can help put more criminals in prison.

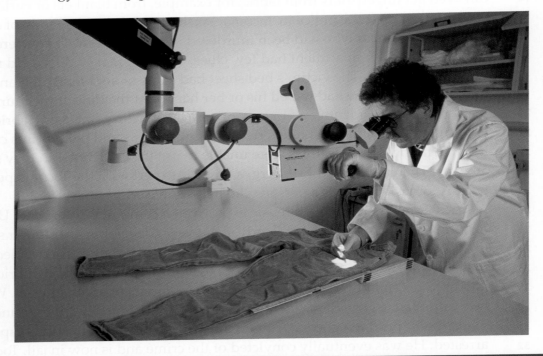

UNIT 3   JUSTICE AND CRIME

Fact-Finding Exercise

Read the passage again. Read the following statements. Check whether they are True or False. If a statement is false, rewrite the statement so that it is true. Then go back to the passage and find the line that supports your answer.

1 _____ True _____ False Fingerprint testing always helps to solve crimes.

_____

2 _____ True _____ False New fingerprint technology can identify body fluids.

_____

3 _____ True _____ False When the woman was murdered in Tacoma, Washington, it was impossible to identify a fingerprint from fabric.

_____

4 _____ True _____ False Eric Berg quickly developed new software to improve photos.

_____

5 _____ True _____ False Eric Berg's technology may help solve older crimes, too.

_____

6 _____ True _____ False The drop of sweat on the scissors was the only clue in the Virginia murder.

_____

7 _____ True _____ False The laser system of lights can only find evidence in the dark.

_____

Reading Analysis

Read each question carefully. Circle the letter or the number of the correct answer, or write your answer in the space provided.

1 What is the main idea of the passage?
  a. New technology always solves every crime, even old ones.
  b. New technology helps solve many crimes, even old ones.
  c. New technology is only useful in solving murders.

2 Read lines 3 and 4.
  a. What are **blood**, **sweat**, and **saliva?**

  _____

  b. How do you know?

  _____

  _____

  c. Why is the word **prints** in quotation marks (" ")?
   1. Because it is an abbreviated form of the word *fingerprints*
   2. Because it is an unusual word in criminal investigation
   3. Because it may be confused with prints of photographs

  d. Whose prints are already on file?
   1. People who have never committed a crime in the past
   2. People who have been convicted of a crime in the past
   3. All the people who live in a city, state, or country

3 Read lines 13 and 14.
  a. What are **blankets** and **curtains?**

  _____

  b. How do you know?

  _____

  _____

4 Read lines 16–18. Which word is a synonym for **clues?**

  _____

5 Read lines 25–27.

   a. What is a **forensic expert?**

      _____

   b. An **expert** is a person who
      1. is very skilled at working with evidence
      2. is very skilled at working with computers
      3. is very skilled at working in a special field

   c. What does **enhance** mean?

      _____

   d. How do you know?

      _____

      _____

6 Read lines 36–39.

   a. In the past, what did the police sometimes do with evidence they could not identify?
      1. They threw it away.
      2. They didn't collect it.
      3. They saved it.

   b. Why did they do this?

      _____

7 Read lines 41–44.

   a. What was the only clue the police had in the 15-year-old murder case?

      _____

   b. What is the purpose of the colon (:) in line 44?
      1. It introduces the clue.
      2. It connects two sentences.
      3. It separates two ideas.

8 Read lines 48–51. What does **previously** mean?
   a. Unfortunately
   b. In the past
   c. Surprisingly

C Information Organization

Read the passage a second time. Underline what you think are the main ideas. Then scan the reading and complete the following chart, using the sentences that you have underlined to help you. You will use this chart later to answer questions about the reading.

Type of Technology	1. Fingerprint Testing	2. DNA Testing	3. Laser Lights
How can it help solve crimes?			
Which crime was it useful for?			
Why was it useful?			

D Information Recall and Summary

Read each question carefully. Use your chart to answer the questions. Do not refer back to the passage. When you are finished, write a brief summary of the reading.

1   a. What can new fingerprint testing identify about a criminal?

_____

_____

_____

_____

b. How is this different from fingerprint testing in the past?

_____

_____

2 Why is it difficult to identify a fingerprint or palm print on fabric?

_____

_____

3 How can new DNA testing help solve the crime in Newport News, Virginia?

_____

_____

4 Why is laser light technology important?

_____

_____

Summary

Work in pairs or alone. Write a brief summary of the reading, and put it on the board. Compare your summary with your classmates'. Which one best describes the main idea of the reading?

_____

_____

_____

_____

_____

_____

_____

Dictionary Skills

Read the following sentences. Use the context to help you understand the boldface words. Read the dictionary entry for that word and circle the appropriate definition. Then rewrite the sentence, using the definition you have chosen. Be sure to make your sentence grammatically correct.

1

> **fabric** *n.* **1** [C; U] cloth, material: *The sofa is covered with a soft cotton fabric.* **2** *fig.* [U] the composition, substance of s.t.: *The fabric of our society has been torn by crime and a bad economy.*

The latest technology can even get fingerprints from **fabric**, for example, blankets or curtains.

_____

2

> **pattern** *n.* **1** an example or model to be followed: *A research paper must follow a specific pattern.* **2** a form or guide to follow when making s.t.: *She made the dress herself from a pattern.* **3** a design of regular shapes and lines: *The flower pattern in that dress is very pretty.* **4** a repeated set of events, characteristics, or features: *There is a pattern to his behavior, in that he grows quiet when he's sad.*

The newest kind of fingerprint testing can do much more than simply record a fingerprint **pattern.**

_____

3

> **scene** *n.* **1 a.** a piece of a film or play, usu. showing one situation: *There is a very exciting chase scene in that movie.* **b.** part of an act: *Let's rehearse Act III, Scene 2.* **2** anger or embarrassing behavior, often in public: *She made a scene at the party by drinking too much and falling into the swimming pool.* **3** a place where s.t. happens: *the crime scene* **4** a view of s.t., especially from a specific place: *She won a prize for her photo of a country scene.* **5 behind the scenes: a.** offstage: *The actor plays a nice man, but behind the scenes he is very cruel.* **b.** in a less obvious or secret place: *Not many people know what happens behind the scenes at the White House.* **6 to set the scene:** to make ready, prepare: *It is usually true that a happy childhood sets the scene for a happy future.*

In all crimes, detectives carefully take samples of evidence from the **scene.**

_____

F Word Forms

PART 1

In English, some verbs change to nouns by adding -ment—for example, *arrange (v.), arrangement (n.)*. Complete each sentence with a correct form of the words on the left. **Use the correct tense of the verb in either the affirmative or the negative. Use the singular or plural form of the noun.**

improve (v.)

improvement (n.)

1. Criminologists have made many _____ in the ways they now solve crimes. Criminologists _____ the accuracy of their work only to catch criminals. They also try to help prove that some suspects are innocent, too.

enhance (v.)

enhancement (n.)

2. Jane put on her makeup very carefully. She believes that makeup _____ her appearance. Sam doesn't think that Jane's appearance needs _____. He thinks she's very pretty without makeup.

enforce (v.)

enforcement (n.)

3. One of a police officer's jobs is law _____. A police officer not only _____ the law, but also tries to help prevent crimes from happening.

develop (v.)

development (n.)

4. Many people work for years on the effective _____ of new computer software. People usually _____ simple software programs. They prefer to work on complex and powerful software programs.

require (v.)

requirement (n.)

5. Michelle wanted to work for a new company, but the company _____ a Master's degree in business, and she didn't have one. Michelle returned to school and studied for her Master's degree in order to meet the company's education _____.

In English, the verb and noun forms of some words are the same—for example, *help (n.)* and *help (v.)*. Complete each sentence with the correct form of the word on the left. **Use the correct tense of the verb in either the affirmative or the negative form. Use the singular or plural form of the noun. In addition, indicate whether you are using the noun (n.) or verb (v.) form.**

witness

1 When a couple gets married, they need to have

_____ who attend the marriage ceremony. The
(n., v.)

people who _____ the marriage ceremony sign
(n., v.)

their names on a legal document.

file

2 The police keep _____ on all convicted criminals.
(n., v.)

They have fingerprints, photographs, and other information

about each person. They _____ the information
(n., v.)

in unlocked cabinets. They keep the information carefully

locked away.

murder

3 The law classifies _____ into several categories,
(n., v.)

depending on whether the killing was planned, unplanned,

or accidental, for example. Every _____ is carefully
(n., v.)

investigated.

arrest

④ Tomorrow the police _____ a suspect in a "white
  _(n., v.)_
collar" crime. The person is suspected of stealing company

secrets and selling them to another company. The number

of _____ involving white collar crime has increased
  _(n., v.)_

dramatically in recent years.

record

⑤ Doctors and dentists _____ their patients' health
  _(n., v.)_
history for permanent reference. Such health _____
  _(n., v.)_

can be very helpful.

Word Partnership	Use _record_ with:
n.	record **a song**
	record **album**, record **club**, record
	company, **hit** record, record **industry**,
	record **label**, record **producer**, record **store**,
	record **earnings**, record **high**, record **low**,
	record **numbers**, record **temperatures**,
	record **time**, **world** record,
v.	**break a** record, **set a** record

G Vocabulary in Context

arrests (n.)	evidence (n.)	pattern (n.)
clues (n.)	experts (n.)	scene (n.)
criminologists (n.)	fabric (n.)	
enforce (v.)	file (v.)	

Read the sentences below. Complete each blank space with the correct word from the list above. Use each word only once.

1 Police officers, detectives, and many other people _____ the law in a variety of ways.

2 Much _____ is required in order to identify a suspect and solve a crime.

3 We always _____ our important documents in a safe place.

4 Michael wanted to ask Jane to marry him. The _____ he chose for his proposal was the restaurant where they had dinner together for the first time.

5 _____ such as hair and skin provide very good evidence for identifying crime suspects.

6 The complex _____ on that carpet is very attractive.

7 Some mechanics are _____ at finding out what is wrong with a car.

8 Cotton is a very cool _____ to wear in the heat of the summer.

9 _____ are very skilled at solving crimes.

UNIT 3 JUSTICE AND CRIME

10 The police can only make _____ when they have enough evidence to suspect someone of having committed a crime.

Critical Thinking Strategies

Read the following questions and think about the answers. Write your answer below each question. Then compare your answers with those of your classmates.

1 Eric Berg used his own time and money to improve crime scene photos. Why do you think he worked so hard at this? What might be some reasons?

_____

_____

_____

2 The fingerprints of convicted criminals are kept on file permanently, but not the fingerprints of everyone. Should everyone's fingerprints be taken and kept on file permanently? Why or why not?

_____

_____

_____

Topics for Discussion and Writing

1 In the United States, the fingerprints of convicted criminals are kept on file permanently. Do you agree with this? Or do you think the fingerprints should not be on file after the criminal comes out of jail? Why? Explain your opinion.

2 Criminal investigators try to collect as much evidence as they can in order to identify the person who committed a crime. How much evidence does a jury need in order to convict a person of a crime?

3 Many people's fingerprints are not on file. As a result, criminal investigators cannot always use fingerprints they find at the scene of a crime. These fingerprints may not be on file. Should the law require all people to put their fingerprints on file, even if they have never committed a crime? Explain your reasons for your answer.

4 **Write in your journal.** Chapter 9 discusses some new kinds of technology to help solve crimes. Which new technology do you think is the most important one? Why? What types of crimes do you think it can help solve?

J Follow-Up Activities

1 Each person's fingerprints are unique and do not change over the person's lifetime. Scientists studied fingerprint patterns and developed a system for classifying them by type in order to make identification more accurate. Examine the sample fingerprints below.

Figure 1: Arch

Figure 2: Left loop

Figure 3: Right loop

Figure 4: Tent

Figure 5: Whorl

On a separate sheet of paper, make your own fingerprint and compare it to the samples. Which pattern does your fingerprint have? How is it similar to that pattern? What are the differences that make it clear they are not the same fingerprint? When you have finished, be sure to destroy the paper with your fingerprint on it.

2 Go to www.nist.gov/public-affairs/licweb/fingerprints.htm and examine the sample prints. Then do the fingerprint matching game. See if you can identify the print taken from a crime scene.

3 Read the line graph below. Answer the questions that follow.

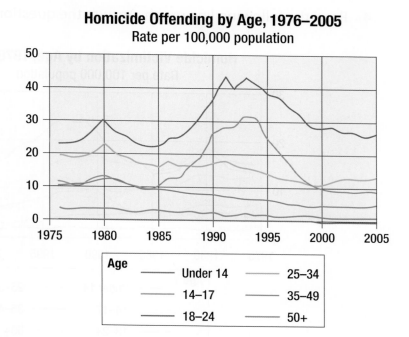

Homicide Offending by Age, 1976–2005
Rate per 100,000 population

Age
— Under 14   — 25–34
— 14–17   — 35–49
— 18–24   — 50+

a. Who is an offender?
    1. The person who is killed
    2. The killer

b. In which five-year period were the most homicides committed?
    1. 1985–1990
    2. 1990–1995
    3. 1995–2000
    4. 2000–2005

c. For all five-year time periods, how old is the person most likely to have committed a homicide? _____

d. For all five-year time periods, how old is the person least likely to have committed a homicide? _____

e. What can we conclude from this graph?
   1. As people get older, they are more likely to commit a homicide.
   2. As people get older, they are less likely to commit a homicide.
   3. As people get older, they are still equally likely to commit a homicide.

4 Read the following line graph. Answer the questions that follow.

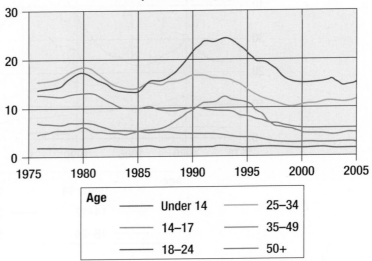

Homicide Victimization by Age, 1976–2005
Rate per 100,000 population

a. Who is a victim?
   1. The person who is killed
   2. The killer

b. From 1980 to 2000, what can you understand about the age of a homicide victim?
   1. Most victims were over 50 years old.
   2. Most victims were between the ages of 25–34.
   3. Most victims were between the ages of 18–24.

c. For the 30-year time period indicated on the chart, what can you understand about the age of homicide victims?
   1. The age of most homicide victims has gotten younger.
   2. The age of most homicide victims has gotten older.
   3. The age of most homicide victims has stayed the same.

K Cloze Quiz

Read the passage below. Fill in the blanks with one word from the list. Use each word only once.

additional	criminals	fabric	matched
apparent	efficiently	file	reveal
arrested	enhance	fluids	solved
clues	evidence	helpful	technology
crime	expert	identify	witnesses

Solving crimes is one of the most important jobs of law enforcement. Improvements in _____ technology help detectives solve crimes faster, (1)
and more _____, today. For example, crime labs have new kinds of (2)
DNA testing, which can identify body _____ such as blood, sweat, and (3)
saliva. There are also new kinds of fingerprint testing. In the past, fingerprint testing was only _____ if the fingerprints from the crime scene could (4)
be _____ with "prints" that were already on file. The fingerprints of (5)
convicted _____ are kept on file in police records permanently. People (6)
whose fingerprints are not on _____ cannot be identified in this way, (7)
and as a result, many crimes have not been _____. (8)

However, the newest kind of fingerprint testing can do much more than simply record a fingerprint pattern. It can provide _____ (9) information about a fingerprint, such as the age and sex of its owner. The fingerprints can _____ (10) if the person takes medication, too. But the latest _____ (11) does even more. It can even get fingerprints from _____ (12), for example, blankets or curtains.

In a recent case, the police in Tacoma, Washington, found the body of a 27-year-old woman who had been murdered in her bedroom. There were no _____ (13), and her apartment had few _____ (14). The only real evidence did not seem very helpful. The victim's bed sheet had some of her blood on it and looked as if someone had wiped his hands. At the time of the murder, it was impossible to _____ (15) a fingerprint from fabric. The detectives were unable to use the _____ (16), but they saved it anyway. Then they called Eric Berg. He was not only a forensic expert, but a computer _____ (17), too. He had spent years developing computer software in his own home to _____ (18), or improve, crime scene photos. Eric Berg had used his computer to make the palm print more _____ (19), or clear. When he was done, he gave the evidence to the detectives. The detectives found a man whose palm print matched a print on file. Only two hours later the suspect was _____ (20). He was eventually convicted of the crime and is now in jail.

Crossword Puzzle

Read the clues on the next page. Write the answers in the correct spaces in the puzzle.

Crossword Puzzle Clues

ACROSS CLUES

3. During a trial, people give _____. They say what they saw or know about the case.
5. If a person is _____ of a crime, the jury acquits him.
8. _____ is money that the suspect gives the court to ensure that he or she will appear in court again.
10. If a person is proven _____, then she is convicted.
12. However; nevertheless
14. An error
19. Improve; make better
20. There are different types of _____ for a crime; for example, fines, probation, and time in prison.
21. Need
23. In the past; before
25. A _____ is a person who saw a crime take place.

DOWN CLUES

1. The word _____ is an abbreviated form of the word *fingerprints*.
2. I like to write with a _____. I don't like pencils.
4. An _____ is a person who is skilled in a particular area.
6. The jury needs strong _____ to prove that a suspect really committed a crime.
7. Blood, saliva, and sweat are all body _____.
8. The police record the charges against a suspect at the police station. They _____ the suspect.
9. A _____ is the person a crime is committed against.
11. Dependability
13. Cloth such as a blanket, curtains, or clothing
15. _____ is the punishment that a judge gives a convicted person.
16. **I**, _____; **he**, **him**
17. Part of a police officer's job is to _____ the law.
18. If a suspect cannot afford a lawyer, the judge may _____ one.
22. The opposite of **yes**
24. The opposite of **down**

1. The three chapters in this unit all discuss an aspect of crime. Chapter 7 outlines how a suspect is arrested and charged with a crime. Chapter 8 describes how an innocent man was convicted as a result of eyewitnesses' mistakes. Chapter 9 discusses how modern technology can help solve crimes.

   a. Should lawmakers and the courts consider such factors as a criminal's home life, age, and physical condition when making laws and punishing convicted criminals?

   _____

   _____

   _____

   _____

   _____

   b. Can courts ensure that eyewitnesses have not made mistakes? If so, how?

   _____

   _____

   _____

   _____

   _____

   c. How much evidence is needed in order to convict a suspect of a crime and be sure the guilty person is truly guilty?

   _____

   _____

   _____

   _____

   _____

Science and History

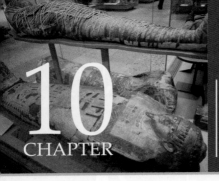

10 CHAPTER

Ancient Artifacts and Ancient Air

Prereading Preparation

1. What kind of work do archeologists perform?

   _____

   _____

2. What do archeologists study in order to learn about the past?

   _____

3. What can archeological discoveries tell us about the past?

   _____

4. Where would you find ancient air?

   _____

   _____

5 How can ancient air help us learn about the past? About the future?

_____

_____

Track 10

Ancient Artifacts and Ancient Air

1   Archeologists made an exciting discovery in Egypt in 1954. During an
2 excavation near the base of the Great Pyramid, they uncovered an ancient crypt.
3 Although they believed that this discovery would help us understand Egypt's past,
4 they also hoped that it would give us important information about the future.
5   This crypt was a tomb, or burial place, for a dead Egyptian pharaoh, or king.
6 Historians believed that the Egyptians buried their pharaohs with two boats: one
7 to carry the body and the other to carry the soul. This was one of their religious
8 customs about death. The archeologists expected to find two boats inside the
9 crypt. As they broke the crypt open, they smelled the scent of wood. The ancient
10 Egyptians had sealed the room so effectively that the aroma of the cedar wood was
11 still preserved. Inside the crypt, archeologists found a 4,600-year-old boat that was
12 in almost perfect condition. In addition, they found another closed room next to the
13 crypt. Archeologists and historians believed that this chamber contained the second
14 boat. If so, archeologists would have better information about the past. They would
15 be sure about the religious custom of burying pharaohs with two boats.
16   However, this was not the only information they hoped to find. They
17 wondered if the air in the two rooms contained something special that helped
18 to preserve the wood. This information could help in the preservation of
19 ancient artifacts in museums throughout the world. Researchers also hoped
20 to find some answers about the future by carefully examining the air in the
21 second chamber. When the archeologists opened the first chamber, all the
22 old air escaped. Scientists wanted to recover the air in the second chamber,
23 compare it with the air of the present, and then examine the differences,
24 especially differences in the level of carbon dioxide (CO_2). This information
25 might help them predict changes in the air in the future. They also did not want
26 outside air to get inside the chamber. Careful planning would be necessary in
27 order to open the second room and save the air. In fact, it took years to plan
28 the excavation and to design and make the equipment necessary to open the
29 chamber and collect the air inside.

30 Finally, in October 1986 an international team of scientists, using special
31 equipment, drilled through the roof of the chamber. The hole they made was
32 kept carefully sealed. As they broke into the ancient room, they realized that the
33 chamber was not sealed. They took an air sample. The air inside was the same as
34 the air outside. The scientists were very disappointed. However, they continued
35 working to see what was inside the chamber. The team lowered a light and a
36 camera into the small hole, and looked at the interior of the room on a television
37 monitor. The second boat was really there!

38 After the scientists took samples of the air inside the chamber and photographed
39 it completely, they sealed up the hole in the roof and left the room as they had
40 found it. Although they did not get samples of 4,600-year-old air, they did confirm
41 the Egyptian custom of burying pharaohs with two boats. More importantly, they
42 practiced a new, non-destructive approach to archeology: investigate an ancient
43 location, photograph it, and leave it untouched. When archeologists opened the
44 first chamber, they removed the boat. The Egyptian government built a museum
45 on the site for the first boat. During the construction of the museum, the vibrations
46 from the heavy machinery disturbed the second room and probably destroyed
47 the seal. Water leaked in, too, so the second boat was not as well preserved as the
48 first boat.

49 The investigation of the second chamber taught archeologists a valuable
50 lesson. New excavations will not only use modern technology, but they will also
51 follow the idea of preserving the entire location for future studies.

UNIT 4   SCIENCE AND HISTORY

Fact-Finding Exercise

Read the passage again. Read the following statements. Check whether they are True or False. If a statement is false, rewrite the statement so that it is true. Then go back to the passage and find the line that supports your answer.

1 _____ True _____ False   Archeological discoveries give us information about the past.

_____

2 _____ True _____ False   Archeologists recently discovered a body in a crypt in Egypt.

_____

3 _____ True _____ False   Archeologists found a boat in the second crypt near the Great Pyramids.

_____

4 _____ True _____ False   Archeologists have not opened the second room yet.

_____

5 _____ True _____ False   There is no old air left in the second chamber.

_____

6 _____ True _____ False   The investigation team went inside the second chamber.

_____

7 _____ True _____ False   The Egyptian government is going to put the second boat in a museum.

_____

Reading Analysis

Read each question carefully. Circle the letter or the number of the correct answer, or write your answer in the space provided.

1 What is the main idea of the passage?

    a. Analyzing old air is important because it helps us understand the future and preserve ancient artifacts.

    b. A recent archeological discovery helped us understand the future and the past and introduced new technology.

    c. Archeologists recently discovered a crypt near the Great Pyramid in Egypt, and they carefully examined it.

2 In line 3, what is the purpose of **although?**

    a. It introduces two different ideas.

    b. It introduces two similar ideas.

    c. It introduces two new ideas.

3 In line 5, what is a **crypt?**

_____

4 In line 5, what is a synonym for **pharaoh?**

_____

5 Read lines 6 and 7. What is the purpose of the colon (:)?

    a. It shows that the sentence continues for another line.

    b. It connects two sentences and makes them one sentence.

    c. It introduces the purpose of the two boats.

6 In line 9, what does **as** mean?

    a. Before

    b. Like

    c. When

7 In line 10, what does **sealed** mean?

    a. Locked with a key

    b. Closed completely

    c. Hidden carefully

8 Read lines 11–14.

   a. What comes after **in addition?**

     1. More information
     2. The same information
     3. The result of the previous information

   b. What does **chamber** mean?

     1. Crypt
     2. Room
     3. Historian

   c. What does **if so** mean?

     1. If the second chamber really contained a second boat
     2. If archeologists could be sure of the Egyptian custom
     3. If there was really a second chamber next to the crypt

9 In line 16, why is **however** used at the beginning of the paragraph?

   a. To show that the paragraph gives the same information as the paragraph before it

   b. To show that the paragraph gives different information from the paragraph before it

10 Read lines 22–24.

   a. What does CO_2 represent?

     1. An abbreviation
     2. An amount
     3. A chemical symbol

   b. What is CO_2?

_____

   c. How do you know?

_____

11 Read lines 26–29. What is the purpose of **in fact?**

   a. To give true information
   b. To emphasize the previous information
   c. To introduce different information

12 Read lines 40 and 41.

    a. What is the purpose of **did** in **they did confirm the Egyptian custom of burying pharaohs with two boats?**

        1. To form a question
        2. To show the past
        3. To give emphasis

    b. What does **confirm** mean?

        1. See
        2. Prove
        3. Write

13 Read lines 41–43. What is the purpose of the colon (:)?

    a. It shows that the sentence continues for another line.
    b. It connects two sentences and makes them one sentence.
    c. It introduces the new non-destructive approach to archeology.

14 Read lines 50 and 51: "New excavations will not only use modern technology, but they will also follow the idea of preserving the entire location for future studies." What is a synonym for **not only . . . but also?**

    a. And
    b. But
    c. So

UNIT 4 SCIENCE AND HISTORY

Information Organization

Read the passage again. Underline what you think are the main ideas. Then scan the reading and complete the following outline, using the sentences that you have underlined to help you. You will use this outline later to answer questions about the reading.

I. Archeological Discovery in Egypt
   A. Date:
   B. Place:
   C. The Discovery:

II. Historians' Belief about Egyptian Burial Customs
   A.
   B. The Purpose of the Boats:

III. The Excavation of the Crypt
   A.
   B.
   C.

IV. What the Archeologists and Historians Hoped to Learn
   A. Information about the Past:
   B. Information about Preserving Wood:
   C. Information about the Future:

V. The Excavation of the Second Chamber
   A. Date:
   B. Method of Excavation:
      1.
      2.
      3.
      4.

VI. The Significance of the Second Excavation
   A.
   B. They practiced a new, non-destructive approach to archeology:
      1.
      2.
      3.
   C. They found out that when the Egyptian government built a museum for the first boat, vibrations from the machinery disturbed the second room and destroyed the seal.

Information Recall and Summary

Read each question carefully. Use your outline to answer the questions. Do not refer back to the passage. When you are finished, write a brief summary of the reading.

1 Where and when did archeologists discover the crypt?

_____

2 What was the purpose of the crypt?

_____

3 What is an ancient Egyptian religious custom about death?

_____

4 Why was the second chamber so important to historians?

_____

_____

5 How did researchers hope to find answers about the future in the second chamber?

_____

_____

6 **a.** Why did it take such a long time before the team opened the second chamber?

_____

b. How was the excavation of the second chamber different from the excavation of the first chamber?

_____

7 How did the air in the second chamber escape?

_____

_____

8 What did the team do after they opened and photographed the second chamber?

_____

Summary

Work in pairs or alone. Write a brief summary of the reading, and put it on the board. Compare your summary with your classmates'. Which one best describes the main idea of the reading?

_____

_____

_____

E

Dictionary Skills

Read the following sentences. Use the context to help you understand the boldface words. Read the dictionary entry for that word and circle the appropriate definition. Then rewrite the sentence, using the definition you have chosen. Be sure to make your sentence grammatically correct.

1

> **base** _n._ **1** the lower part of s.t., foundation: _That vase is on a wooden base._ **2** the point where a part of s.t. is connected to the whole: _The boxer hit the base of his opponent's neck._ **3** s.t. (a fact, an assumption, etc.) from which a start is made: _We will begin with your salary as a base and give you a 5 percent increase._ **4** the main place where one works or lives, (_syn._) headquarters: _They use their apartment in New York as a home base from which they travel frequently._ **5** (in chemistry) a bitter-tasting substance that turns litmus paper blue **6** a military camp, building, airport, etc.: _The Air Force planes flew back to their base._ **7** (in baseball) one of four squares touched by runners **8** _infrml._ **to get to first base: a.** to start: _He tried to get a new job but did not get to first base._ **b.** _slang_ to kiss **9** _infrml._ **off base:** wrong: _She is off base in her ideas about what is wrong with the economy._ **10** _infrml._ **to touch all the bases:** (from baseball) to address all major points: _He touched all the bases in his talk about the new product._

In 1954, archeologists uncovered an ancient crypt near the **base** of the Great Pyramid.

_____

2 **custom** *n.* **1** [C; U] a habitual way of behaving that is special to a person, people, region, or nation: *It is his custom to smoke a cigar after dinner.* || *It is British custom to drink tea at four o'clock each afternoon.* **2** **customs** taxes on goods brought into a country, (*syn.*) duties: *I paid the customs on some wine and perfume from France.* **3** *used with a sing. v.* **customs** the branch of government and its workers who keep track of the goods brought into a country: *I had to go through customs when I came to this country.*

The ancient Egyptians had a religious **custom.** They buried their pharaohs with two boats: one to carry the body and the other to carry the soul.

_____

_____

3 **escape** *v.* [I; T] -caped, -caping, -capes **1** to get away (from prison or another place of confinement): *The lion escaped from its cage.* **2** to get free temporarily: *We escaped to an island in the Pacific for our vacation.* **3** to manage to stay free of, to avoid: *He escaped military service because of his bad eyesight.* **4** [T] to resist one's efforts to remember: *Her name escapes me at the moment.*

The air **escaped** from the second chamber at the time the museum was built for the first boat.

_____

_____

4 **lower** *adj. comp. of* low *v.* **1** [T] to let down to a reduced level or position: *A sailor lowered a rope over the side of the ship.* **2** [I; T] to make less in amount, degree, or intensity: *The dealer lowered the price of the car.* **3** **to lower oneself:** to act beneath one's dignity or self-respect: *He needed money but would not lower himself to picking up coins on the street.*

The scientists **lowered** a light and a camera into the second chamber.

_____

_____

Word Forms

In English, verbs change to nouns in several ways. Some verbs become nouns by adding the suffix *-ion* or *-ation*—for example, *preserve (v.)* becomes *preservation (n.)*. Complete each sentence with the correct form of the words on the left. **Use the correct tense of the verb in either the affirmative or the negative form. Use the singular or plural form of the noun.**

predict *(v.)*   1   The weather forecast _____ snow for last night, but

prediction *(n.)*   it snowed anyway. The _____ about the weather

was incorrect.

correct *(v.)*   2   After our teacher assigns an essay, he always _____

correction *(n.)*   the papers. If there are only a few _____, the

students get good grades.

excavate *(v.)*   3   The _____ of King Tut's tomb was an important and

excavation *(n.)*   famous event. Archeologists _____ this tomb in

Egypt in the 1920s.

examine *(v.)*   4   The doctor's _____ of the sick child will take a

examination *(n.)*   long time. The doctor _____ the sick child until

tomorrow to find out what is wrong.

inform *(v.)*   5   The teacher _____ us about the TOEFL right now.

information *(n.)*   This _____ will be very helpful to all of us.

In English, verbs change to nouns in several ways. Some verbs become nouns by adding the suffix *-y*—for example, *embroider (v.)* becomes *embroidery (n.)*. Complete each sentence with the correct form of the words on the left. **Use the correct tense of the verb in either the affirmative or the negative form. Use the singular or plural form of the noun.**

recover *(v.)*
recovery *(n.)*

1 John's boat sank in the middle of a deep lake. However, he _____ it with the help of some friends. The difficult _____ took several hours.

discover *(v.)*
discovery *(n.)*

2 An important _____ that may take place soon is the cure for cancer. Researchers _____ a cure for cancer in the near future.

master *(v.)*
mastery *(n.)*

3 After studying English for four years, Angela finally _____ the language. Her _____ of English helped her get a higher paying job.

inquire *(v.)*
inquiry *(n.)*

4 When Marla arrived at the airport, she _____ about flights to Paris and to London. Marla made both _____ at the Information Desk.

deliver *(v.)*
delivery *(n.)*

5 The letter carrier _____ the mail early every morning. She comes in the afternoon. I am excited about the _____ because I am waiting for information about my college application.

Word Partnership	Use *deliver* with:
n.	deliver **a letter,** deliver **mail,** deliver **a message,** deliver **news,** deliver **a package,** deliver **a lecture,** deliver **a speech,** deliver **a baby,** deliver **a blow**

G Vocabulary in Context

although (conj.)	excavation (n.)	in fact	sealed (adj.)
custom (n.)	if so	predict (v.)	
discovered (v.)	in addition	recover (v.)	

Read the following sentences. Complete each blank space with the correct word or phrase from the list above. Use each word or phrase only once.

1. _____ I am sick, I can't stay home. I have to go to work anyway.

2. Debbie is doing very well in college. _____, she got 100% on her last five tests and an A+ on her research paper.

3. In the United States, it is a _____ for people to shake hands when they first meet.

4. Today, bottles and cans in stores are carefully _____ to prevent air and germs from getting inside.

5. The supermarket may be open late tonight. _____, I will go shopping after work instead of early tomorrow morning.

6. During the _____ of an old building, construction workers found some ancient artifacts.

7. English students must study grammar. _____, they must study reading, writing, and listening comprehension.

8. Tommy left his sweater in the cafeteria. Fortunately, he was able to _____ it at the Lost and Found Office.

9. Some people go to fortune tellers, who use cards in order to _____ what the future will be.

10. Christopher Columbus _____ America in 1492. Before Columbus found America, most people did not know about its existence.

Critical Thinking Strategies

Read the following questions and think about the answers. Write your answer below each question. Then compare your answers with those of your classmates.

1 After the archeologists opened the second chamber and took pictures, they sealed it up again. Why did they close it again?

_____

_____

2 What are some other ways that archeologists can preserve important historical sites during and after excavations?

_____

_____

_____

Topics for Discussion and Writing

1 **a.** How do archeological discoveries help us understand the past?

_____

_____

_____

b. Why is understanding the past important?

_____

_____

_____

2 How can the analysis of ancient air be important?

_____

_____

3 a. Do you think it is important not to disturb ancient locations? Why or why not?

_____

_____

_____

   b. Are there times when it is better to remove ancient artifacts and take them to a museum? When?

_____

_____

_____

4 **Write in your journal.** The archeological team left the second boat in the chamber and sealed it again. Do you think it would be better to put the second boat in a museum, too? Why or why not?

J

Follow-Up Activity

In groups of three or four, form a panel of experts. Someone has discovered the ruins of an ancient city in your country. Your government wants to investigate this site and has asked your panel to plan the excavation. In your group, decide who you will need to help you with this project. Plan the work that your group will do at this location. Decide which artifacts you will take away to a museum and which ones you will leave at the site. When you are finished, compare your plan with your classmates' plans. As a class, decide which plans the government should use.

_____

_____

_____

_____

_____

Cloze Quiz

Read the passage below. Fill in the blanks with one word from the list. Use each word only once.

addition	compare	excavations	museum
air	crypt	fact	predict
although	custom	however	recover
ancient	discovery	information	sealed
chamber	examining	king	so

Archeologists made an exciting _____ (1) in Egypt in 1954. During an excavation near the base of the Great Pyramid, they uncovered an ancient crypt. Although they believed that this discovery would help us understand Egypt's past, they also hoped that it would give us important _____ (2) about the future.

This _____ (3) was a tomb, or burial place, for a dead Egyptian pharaoh, or _____ (4). Historians believed that the Egyptians buried their pharaohs with two boats: one to carry the body and another to carry the soul. This was one of their religious customs about death. The archeologists expected to find two boats inside the crypt. As they broke the crypt open, they smelled the scent of wood. The ancient Egyptians had sealed the room so effectively that the aroma of the cedar wood was still preserved. Inside the crypt, archeologists found a 4,600-year-old boat that was in almost perfect condition. In _____ (5), they found another closed room next to the crypt. Archeologists and historians believed that this chamber contained the second boat. If _____ (6), archeologists would have better information about the past. They would be sure about the religious _____ (7) of burying pharaohs with two boats.

_____ (8), this was not the only information they hoped to find. They wondered if the air in the two rooms contained something special that helped to preserve the wood. This information could help in the preservation of _____ (9) artifacts in museums throughout the world. Researchers also hoped to find some answers about the future by carefully _____ (10) the air in the second chamber. When the archeologists opened the first chamber, all the old air escaped. Scientists wanted to _____ (11) the air in the second chamber, _____ (12) it with the air of the present, and then examine the differences, especially differences in the level of carbon dioxide (CO_2). This information might help them _____ (13) changes in the air in the future. They also did not want outside air to get inside the chamber. Careful planning would be necessary in order to open the second room and save the air. In _____ (14), it took years to plan the excavation and to design and make the equipment necessary to open the chamber and collect the air inside.

Finally, in October 1986 an international team of scientists, using special equipment, drilled through the roof of the chamber. The hole they made was kept carefully _____ (15). As they broke into the ancient room, they realized that the chamber was not sealed. They took an air sample. The _____ (16) inside was the same as the air outside. Then the team lowered a light and a camera into the small hole and looked at the interior of the room on a television monitor. The second boat was really there!

After the scientists took samples of the air inside the _____ (17) and photographed it completely, they sealed up the hole in the roof and left the room as they had found it. _____ (18) they did not get samples of 4,600-year-old air, they did learn that the Egyptian custom of burying pharaohs with two boats is true. They also practiced a new, non-destructive approach to archeology: investigate an ancient location, photograph it, and leave it untouched. When archeologists opened the first chamber, they removed the boat. The Egyptian government built a _____ on the site

(19)

for the first boat. During the construction of the museum, the vibrations from the heavy machinery disturbed the second room and probably destroyed the seal. Water leaked in, too, so the second boat was not as well preserved as the first boat.

The investigation of the second chamber taught archeologists a valuable lesson. New _____ will not only use modern technology, but they will

(20)

also follow the idea of preserving the entire location for future studies.

Medical Technology: Saving Lives with Robotics

Prereading Preparation

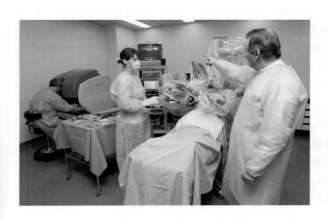

1 What is surgery? Why is surgery performed? Where is surgery performed?

_____

_____

2 Examine both photographs and look at the title of the chapter. How many people are in the operating room in the first picture? How many are in the second picture? Who are these people?

_____

_____

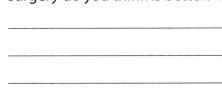

3 Which picture has fewer people? Why are there fewer people?

_____

_____

4 Look at the two photos again. Which kind of surgery do you think is better? Why?

_____

_____

_____

_____

Medical Technology: Saving Lives with Robotics

1   In most operating rooms today, there are two or three surgeons, an
2   anesthesiologist, several nurses, and the patient. All of these people are needed
3   for even a simple surgery. In fact, most surgeries require about a dozen people in
4   the room. This, however, might possibly change in the very near future. Surgical
5   robots may replace several surgeons during one operation. In a few hospitals
6   today, an operation needs only one surgeon, a computer and a surgical robot.
7   Looking even further into the future, the surgeon may not have to be there at all!
8   Robotic surgery has many advantages. It can be less traumatic for the patient.
9   For example, during traditional heart surgery, the surgeon must open the
10 patient's chest in order to perform the operation. Often, the opening, or incision,
11 is about one foot (30 cm) long. However, with the newest robotic surgery, called
12 the da Vinci system, it's possible to make only three or four small incisions—
13 about an inch (about two centimeters) each—instead. Because the incisions are
14 so much smaller, the patient experiences much less pain and bleeding. As a
15 result, he can recover much faster. The da Vinci system is also an improvement
16 in another way. Robotic surgery can be performed more quickly than traditional
17 surgery, which means the surgeons are not so exhausted when they're finished.
18   During the robotic surgery, the doctor controls the robotic "arms" using a
19 computer. Currently, the doctor must be in the operating room with the patient for
20 the robotic systems to react instantly to the doctor's hand movements. However,
21 the doctor does not have to be right next to the patient. In fact, he can actually be
22 a few feet away. With further developments in this technology, the doctor will be
23 able to control the robot from another room. When that becomes possible, it's only
24 a matter of time before the doctor does not have to even be in the same hospital,
25 or even the same state, as the patient. This would allow surgeons to perform
26 operations on patients miles away—even hundreds of miles!
27   Michael Troy strongly believes that the da Vinci robotic surgery system saved
28 his life. He was a 22-year-old college student when he learned that he had
29 kidney cancer. The news was devastating. "I thought this was the end for me,"
30 Michael said. "Many doctors did not want to perform surgery on me because
31 my cancer was so severe. They would have to make a huge incision in my back
32 in order to remove my kidney." Then one of Michael's doctors suggested that
33 Michael might have one other option. He sent Michael to see Dr. Fuentes at
34 Queens Memorial Hospital in Clemens, Missouri. Dr. Fuentes said to Michael,
35 "I think I can save your kidney." At first, Michael did not believe the doctor.

36 "Of course I was skeptical," Michael says. Then Dr. Fuentes told Michael about
37 the da Vinci robot. Dr. Fuentes explained that in order to remove the cancer
38 and save Michael's kidney, he would need four hands to get into the small
39 area. However, the da Vinci robot, under Dr. Fuentes' control, could effectively
40 perform the surgery making only small incisions to Michael's body.
41   Dr. Fuentes showed Michael a video of the da Vinci system. "After I watched
42 the video, I knew that this was the best—maybe even the only—possible treatment
43 for me." A week later, Michael had the surgery. As promised, Dr. Fuentes saved a
44 large part of Michael's kidney, and removed the cancer. "This was all due to the
45 da Vinci system," adds Michael. Today, Michael is a healthy college graduate.
46 "I'm so grateful to Dr. Fuentes for saving my life and my kidney," says Michael.
47 "I would recommend the da Vinci system, especially because my tumor was so
48 large. I didn't want to lose a kidney at such a young age."
49   Robotic surgery is still new technology. However, doctors believe there may
50 be even more astonishing technology in the operating rooms of the future:
51 Robot surgeons. At Duke University in North Carolina in the U.S., doctors and
52 scientists are working to develop a robot that can perform surgery by itself.
53 Dr. Steve Smith of Duke University thinks that the technology could reduce the
54 cost and time necessary to complete some surgical procedures. "We keep giving
55 the robot more and more complex tasks," said Dr. Smith. "So far the robot has
56 been able to accomplish these tasks automatically." Many doctors, including
57 Dr. Smith, agree that it will take about ten years before robot surgeons become
58 a reality. Like most medical technology, in the beginning it will likely be more
59 expensive than using a human surgeon. Eventually, doctors hope that the
60 life-saving technology will become widely available and more affordable
61 for all.

Fact-Finding Exercise

Read the passage again. Read the following statements. Check whether they are True or False. If a statement is false, rewrite the statement so that it is true. Then go back to the passage and find the line that supports your answer.

1 _____ True _____ False   During traditional surgery, there may be more than 10 people in the operating room.

_____

2 _____ True _____ False   Traditional surgery is faster than robotic surgery.

_____

3 _____ True _____ False   Patients recover much faster after traditional surgery than they do after robotic surgery.

_____

4 _____ True _____ False   During robotic surgery, doctors use their arms to control the robot.

_____

5 _____ True _____ False   It may be possible in the future for doctors to operate on patients who are far away.

_____

6 _____ True _____ False   Dr. Fuentes believes that robotic surgery saved his life.

_____

7 _____ True _____ False   Robot surgeons may perform operations without doctors in the future.

_____

Reading Analysis

Read each question carefully. Circle the letter or the number of the correct answer, or write your answer in the space provided.

1 What is the main idea of the reading?

   a. Traditional surgery takes longer and can be more difficult than robotic surgery.

   b. In the future, robot surgeons might perform operations by themselves.

   c. Robotic surgery can be more helpful and effective for patients and doctors.

2 Read lines 1–8.

   a. What word is a synonym of **require?**

   _____

   b. What **might possibly change in the very near future?**

     1. The number of surgeons in an operating room

     2. The number of patients in an operating room

     3. The number of days that a patient must stay in the hospital

   c. This might change because

     1. people are healthier today

     2. one surgical robot may replace several surgeons

     3. surgeries today are easier and faster

   d. What does **traumatic** mean?

     1. Shocking and painful

     2. Frightening and worrying

     3. Long and expensive

3 Read line 10.

   a. What is **an opening?**

   _____

   b. How do you know?

   _____

4 Read lines 15–17.

   a. The surgeons are not so exhausted when they're finished because

     1. robotic surgery requires fewer doctors

     2. robotic surgery is easier than traditional surgery

     3. robotic surgery takes less time than traditional surgery

b. Exhausted means

    1. very tired
    2. very busy
    3. very hungry

5   In line 27, what is the da Vinci system?

  a. A robotic surgery system
  b. A kind of traditional surgery
  c. An illness or disease

6   Read lines 27–29. Who is Michael Troy?

  a. A doctor
  b. A robot surgeon
  c. A patient

7   Read lines 29–31. **The news was devastating. "I thought this was the end for me."**

  a. The second sentence means

    1. Michael thought he was going to drop out of college
    2. Michael thought he was going to die
    3. Michael thought he was going to become very sick

  b. Read the first sentence. **Devastating** means

    1. very upsetting
    2. very confusing
    3. very important

8   Read line 36. **"Of course I was skeptical,"** means

  a. Michael did not want the surgery
  b. Michael has kidney cancer
  c. Michael did not believe his doctor

9   Read lines 51 and 52. **Doctors and scientists are working to develop a robot that can perform surgery by itself.** This means that the robot will

  a. do the surgery alone
  b. help the doctors perform the surgery
  c. do operations on the doctors and scientists

10 Read lines 56–58.

    a. **Many doctors, including Dr. Smith, agree that it will take about ten years before robot surgeons become a reality.** This means

        1. Robot surgeons are used today

        2. Dr. Smith developed robot surgeons about 10 years ago

        3. Robot surgeons will be used in about ten years

    b. Like most medical technology, in the beginning it will likely be **more expensive** than using a human surgeon. What is an antonym for **more expensive?**

        1. More affordable

        2. More popular

        3. More effective

Information Organization

Read the passage again. Underline what you think are the main ideas. Then scan the reading and complete the following chart about the differences between traditional surgery and robotic surgery. Use the sentences that you have underlined to help you.

Differences Between:	Traditional Surgery	Robotic Surgery
In the Operating Room:		
Type of Incision:		
Recovery Time:		
In the Future:	⨯	
Michael Troy's Experience:	Why didn't he have traditional surgery?	What were the results of his robotic surgery?

Information Recall and Summary

Read each question carefully. Use your chart to answer the questions. Do not refer back to the passage. When you are finished, write a brief summary of the reading.

1 What are the main differences between traditional surgery and robotic surgery?

a. _____

b. _____

c. _____

2 What is the future of robotic surgery?

_____

_____

3 Which kind of surgery helped Michael Troy? Why?

_____

_____

Summary

Work in pairs or alone. Write a brief summary of the reading, and put it on the board. Compare your summary with your classmates'. Which one best describes the main idea of the reading?

_____

_____

_____

Dictionary Skills

Read the following sentences. Use the context to help you understand the boldface words. Read the dictionary entry for that word and circle the appropriate definition. Then rewrite the sentence, using the definition you have chosen. Be sure to make your sentence grammatically correct.

1

> **recover** *v.* **1** [I] to regain one's health: *He recovered from his illness and is well again.* **2** [T] to get s.t. back, to get control again: *Workers recovered a sunken boat from the lake.* **3** [T] to make up for losses: *The race car driver recovered the time he lost at the start of the race and won.* **4** [T] to put a new cover (new material) on s.t.: *to recover a sofa -adj.* **recoverable.**

Because the incisions are so much smaller, the patient experiences much less pain and bleeding. As a result, he can **recover** much faster.

2

> **react** *v.* [I] **1** to speak or move when s.t. happens: *When he heard the good news, he reacted with a smile.* **2** to act in a different way because of s.o. or s.t.: *The teacher reacted to the student's bad grades by giving him more homework.* **3** (in chemistry) to change because of contact with another chemical: *Oxygen and iron react together to form rust.*

Currently, the doctor must be in the operating room with the patient for the robotic system to **react** instantly to the doctor's hand movements.

3

> **option** *n.* **1** [C; U] a choice, (*syn.*) an alternative: *She has two options: she can stay here or leave.* **2** [C] a right to buy s.t. at a stated price: *He has a 90-day option to buy that house for $170,000.*

Michael said, "They would have to make a huge incision in my back in order to remove my kidney." Then one of Michael's doctors suggested that Michael might have one other **option.**

Word Forms

In English, the verb and noun forms of some words are the same—for example, *need (n.)* and *need (v.)*. Complete each sentence with the correct form of the words on the left. **Use the correct tense of the verb in either the affirmative or the negative form. Use the singular or plural form of the noun. In addition, indicate whether you are using the noun (n.) or the verb (v.) form.**

change

1 When Michael _____ his job, he and his family had to
(n., v.)

move to California. It was a big _____ for everyone.
(n., v.)

need

2 In many countries there is a great _____ for clean
(n., v.)

water. People _____ it for drinking and for cooking.
(n., v.)

experience

3 Barbara went to college in Spain because she wanted to

_____ life in a different country. She had many new
(n., v.)

and exciting _____ there.
(n., v.)

control

4 I use a remote _____ to turn my TV on and off.
(n., v.)

However, it _____ my radio. I must turn that on
(n., v.)

by myself.

end

5 The _____ of the semester will be very sad for
(n., v.)

Kayla because she will miss her classmates when the

class _____.
(n., v.)

In English, verbs become nouns in several ways. Some verbs become nouns by adding the suffix –*ment*, for example, *appoint (v.)* becomes *appointment (n.)*. Complete each sentence with the correct form of the words on the left. **Use the correct tense of the verb in either the affirmative or the negative form. Use the singular or plural form of the noun.**

require *(v.)*

requirement *(n.)*

1 The college _____ all students to have certain immunizations. You cannot attend college without this _____.

move *(v.)*

movement *(n.)*

2 When the bus suddenly _____ yesterday, a passenger fell out of his seat. The unexpected _____ caused him to fall.

improve *(v.)*

improvement *(n.)*

3 Teresa's piano skills _____ every day. Her _____ is a result of her constant practice.

develop *(v.)*

development *(n.)*

4 The _____ of a paragraph is not very hard, but first you need a main idea. After you _____ that, you can write the rest of the paragraph.

treat *(v.)*

treatment *(n.)*

5 Some medical _____ involve surgery because doctors _____ all illnesses with only medicine.

Word Partnership	Use *treatment* with:
v.	**get/receive** treatment, **give** treatment, **undergo** treatment
n.	treatment **of addiction**, **AIDS** treatment, **cancer** treatment, treatment **center**, treatment **of an illness**, treatment **of prisoners**
adj.	**effective** treatment, **medical** treatment, **better** treatment, **equal/unequal** treatment, **fair** treatment, **humane** treatment, **special** treatment

G Vocabulary in Context

affordable *(adj.)*	option *(n.)*	require *(v.)*	surgery *(n.)*
exhausted *(adj.)*	patient *(n.)*	skeptical *(adj.)*	
incision *(n.)*	recover *(v.)*	surgeon *(n.)*	

Read the following sentences. Complete each blank space with the correct word from the list above. Use each word only once.

1. Gloria is _____. She ran 10 miles this morning, and then worked all day.

2. Dr. Mallory is the _____ who will perform the operation this afternoon.

3. Thank you for offering to help me, but I do not _____ any assistance.

4. The nurse took care of the _____, then recorded his condition in a book.

5. Anna is very _____ of John's ability to drive a car. He has had three accidents already this year!

6. That car costs $40,000. It's too expensive for me. I need a more _____ one.

7. The surgeon made a two-inch _____, then continued with the operation.

8. Cynthia has never had _____. In fact, she has never been in a hospital.

9. I am sorry to hear that you are ill. I hope that you _____ very quickly.

10. When you take this exam, you have the _____ of writing it on paper, or on a computer.

Critical Thinking Strategies

Read the following questions and think about the answers. Write your answer below each question. Then compare your answers with those of your classmates.

1 Traditional surgeries require a lot of people in the operating room. Why do you think this is so?

_____

_____

2 Robotic surgery would allow surgeons to perform operations on patients miles away. Do you think a patient would want a surgeon who is so far away? Why or why not?

_____

_____

3 Michael had surgery for his kidney cancer. What other kinds of operations will be possible with robotic surgery?

_____

_____

4 How can modern technology help a surgeon perform an operation that is less dangerous for the patient?

_____

_____

_____

Topics for Discussion and Writing

1 Robotic surgery is new medical technology that can help a lot of people. What is another type of medical technology that helps people? Write about it.

2 Robotics is used for some surgeries. What other uses might there be for robotics in the field of medicine?

3 **Write in your journal.** Describe an experience you, or someone you know, had with a surgical procedure in a hospital. What was the procedure? How was it performed? How quickly did you, or the person you are writing about, recover?

J Follow-Up Activities

1 You are going to interview Michael Troy about his robotic surgery. Make a list of questions for him. Then, exchange your questions with one of your classmates. Pretend that you are Michael Troy, and write answers to your classmates' questions.

_____

_____

_____

_____

_____

_____

_____

_____

_____

_____

_____

_____

2 Choose a medical procedure that interests you. Prepare a report on the procedure. Describe what it is used for, and how it is performed.

_____

_____

_____

_____

_____

_____

Cloze Quiz

Read the passage below. Fill in the blanks with one word or phrase from the list. Use each word or phrase only once.

as a result	in fact	operation	surgeons
computer	incision	patient	surgery
exhausted	instead	perform	surgical
future	needed	robotic	traditional
however	open	smaller	traumatic

In most operating rooms today, there are two or three _____(1), an anesthesiologist, several nurses, and the _____(2). All of these people are _____(3) for even a simple surgery. _____(4), most surgeries require about a dozen people in the room. This, _____(5), might possibly change in the very near future. _____(6) robots may replace several surgeons during one _____(7). In a few hospitals today, an operation needs only one surgeon, a _____(8)_____, and a surgical robot. Looking even further into the _____(9)_____, the surgeon may not have to be there at all!

Robotic _____(10)_____ has many advantages. It can be less _____(11)_____ for the patient. For example, during _____(12)_____ heart surgery, the surgeon must _____(13)_____ the patient's chest in order to _____(14)_____ the operation. Often, the opening, or _____(15)_____, is about one foot (30 cm) long. However, with the newest _____(16)_____ surgery, called the da Vinci system, it's possible to make only three or four small incisions—about an inch (about two centimeters) each—_____(17)_____. Because the incisions are so much _____(18)_____, the patient experiences much less pain and bleeding. _____(19)_____, he can recover much faster. The da Vinci system is also an improvement in another way. Robotic surgery can be performed more quickly than traditional surgery, which means the surgeons are not so _____(20)_____ when they're finished.

12 CHAPTER

Mars: Our Neighbor in Space

Prereading Preparation

1 What do you know about the planet Mars?

_____

2 Do you think life exists on Mars today? Why or why not?

_____

3 How can we find out if there is life on Mars?

_____

4 Why are scientists so interested in exploring Mars?

_____

_____

Mars: Our Neighbor in Space

1   Ever since people first looked up at the night sky, they have been fascinated by
2   the planet Mars. When scientists started using telescopes to try to see the Red Planet,
3   they wondered if there could be life on Mars. However, for hundreds of years, they
4   could only ask questions. There was no way to actually travel to another planet.

5   When space exploration began in the 1960s, many countries sent unmanned
6   spacecraft to Mars to find out everything they could about our nearest planetary
7   neighbor in space. Unfortunately, only half were successful. Twelve missions
8   landed on the surface, but only seven sent information back to Earth.

9   In spite of the numerous failures, astronomers all over the world are hopeful
10 as each Mars mission approaches the Red Planet. For example, *Mars Observer,* an
11 American spacecraft, was scheduled to move into orbit around Mars and begin
12 sending new information back to Earth. *Mars Observer* was going to study the
13 Martian atmosphere and surface. Unfortunately, scientists lost contact with
14 *Mars Observer*, and the mission, which cost $845 million, failed.

15 In contrast, the United States' mission to Mars in 1996 was a great success.
16 *Mars Pathfinder* sent back more images of Mars than all the previous Mars
17 missions combined. More recently, in 2007, the *Mars Reconnaissance Orbiter* sent
18 back to Earth more information than all other Mars missions put together. The
19 *Phoenix Mars Lander*, in 2008, returned an enormous amount of data as well.

20 What kinds of information did the successful Mars missions obtain? In 1976,
21 the *Viking* spacecraft searched for signs of life, but the tests that they performed
22 had negative results. However, scientists wanted to investigate further into
23 the possibility of life on Mars. This was the purpose of the unsuccessful *Mars
24 Observer* mission in 1993.

25 Scientists' interest in the Red Planet is based on an assumption. They believe
26 that 4.5 billion years ago, Mars and Earth began their existence under similar
27 conditions. During the first billion years, liquid water—in contrast to ice—was
28 abundant on the surface of Mars. This is an indication that Mars was much
29 warmer at that time. Mars also had a thicker atmosphere of carbon dioxide
30 (CO_2). Many scientists think it is possible that life began under these favorable
31 conditions. After all, Earth had the same conditions during its first billion
32 years, when life arose. At some point in time, Earth developed an atmosphere
33 that is rich in oxygen, and an ozone layer. Ozone (O_3) is a form of oxygen. The
34 ozone layer protects Earth from harmful ultraviolet light from the sun. While
35 life not only began on Earth, it also survived and became more complex. In
36 contrast, Mars lost its thick atmosphere of carbon dioxide. Ultraviolet radiation
37 intensified. The planet eventually grew colder, and its water froze.

A biologist at NASA (the National Aeronautics and Space Administration), Chris McKay, has suggested three theories about life on Mars. One possibility is that life never developed. A second possibility is that life arose on Mars just as it did on Earth and survived for at least a billion years. The third is that life arose and simple organisms developed. When environmental conditions on Mars changed, life ended.

Since the early missions, spacecraft have mapped the planet's surface and have landed in better locations. The spacecraft have searched for simple life forms (microorganisms) as well as for signs of water. To date, none of the Mars missions has discovered any sure signs of past or present life. Nonetheless, scientists worldwide are not discouraged. If life ever existed on Mars, they believe that future missions might find records of it under sand, or in the ice. They are thrilled with the data they have obtained so far, and are planning a number of missions in the future. These missions might include airplanes or balloons, which can explore many different sites on the planet's surface.

Even if future missions discover no evidence of past or present life on Mars, scientists will look for the answers to other, intriguing questions. How is Earth different from Mars? Why did life develop here on our planet and not on Mars? Are we alone in the universe?

Fact-Finding Exercise

Read the passage again. Read the following statements. Check whether they are True or False. If a statement is false, rewrite the statement so that it is true. Then go back to the passage and find the line that supports your answer.

1 _____ True _____ False The *Mars Observer* mission was successful.

_____

2 _____ True _____ False The *Mars Pathfinder* mission was successful.

_____

3 _____ True _____ False The *Viking* spacecraft found signs of life on Mars.

_____

4 _____ True _____ False Mars and Earth were very similar 4.5 billion years ago.

_____

5 _____ True _____ False Scientists believe there is liquid water on Mars now.

_____

6 _____ True _____ False During their first billion years, Earth and Mars both had a thick atmosphere of carbon dioxide.

_____

7 _____ True _____ False Chris McKay suggested four theories about life on Mars.

_____

8 _____ True _____ False Scientists are planning more missions to Mars.

_____

Reading Analysis

Read each question carefully. Circle the letter or the number of the correct answer, or write your answer in the space provided.

1 What is the main idea of the passage?

    a. NASA biologists have three possible theories about life on Mars.

    b. The United States sent two missions to Mars, but one was unsuccessful.

    c. Scientists have always been interested in the possibility of life on Mars.

2 The author of this article is in favor of sending more spacecraft to Mars.

    a. Yes

    b. No

    c. We don't know

3 In line 2, what does **the Red Planet** refer to?

    a. The sun

    b. Earth

    c. Mars

4 Read lines 5–7.

    a. When did space exploration begin?

        1. 1950–1959

        2. 1960–1969

        3. 1970–1979

    b. What does **our nearest planetary neighbor in space** mean?

        1. The sun

        2. The spacecraft

        3. Mars

5 Read lines 9 and 10.

    a. **In spite of** means

        1. because of

        2. despite

        3. as well as

    b. **Numerous** means

        1. many

        2. a few

        3. some

6 Read lines 12–19. Which missions to Mars were successful?

    a. Mars Observer

    b. Mars Pathfinder

    c. Mars Reconnaissance Orbiter

    d. a, b, and c

    e. only b and c

7 Read lines 13–19.

    a. What does **in contrast** indicate?

        1. Two similar ideas

        2. Two opposite ideas

    b. Which two words show this relationship?

    _____

8 Read lines 22–24.

    a. What was the purpose of the Mars Observer?

    _____

    b. Was it successful?

        1. Yes

        2. No

9 Read lines 25–27. Which of the following statements is true?

    a. Mars is older than Earth.

    b. Earth is older than Mars.

    c. Mars and Earth are the same age.

10 Read lines 27 and 28. **"During the first billion years, liquid water—in contrast to ice—was abundant on the surface of Mars."**

    a. What form does the water on Mars have today?

        1. Liquid

        2. Solid

    b. How do you know?

    _____

11 In lines 29–30 and in line 33, what do CO_2 and O_3 represent?

    a. Chemical symbols

    b. Abbreviations

    c. Amounts

12 **a.** In line 38, what is in parentheses?

      1. An abbreviation

      2. The purpose of NASA

      3. The words that NASA stands for

    b. Why do you think **NASA** is used in the sentence, and **National Aeronautics and Space Administration** is in parentheses?

_____

13 **a.** In lines 45 and 46, what are **microorganisms?**

    _____

    b. Why is **microorganisms** in parentheses?

      1. It is an example.

      2. It is a special word.

      3. It is a foreign word.

14 Read lines 46–51. What is a synonym for **to date?**

_____

C Information Organization

Read the passage again. Underline what you think are the main ideas. Then scan the reading and complete the following chart, using the sentences that you have underlined to help you. You will use this chart later to answer questions about the reading.

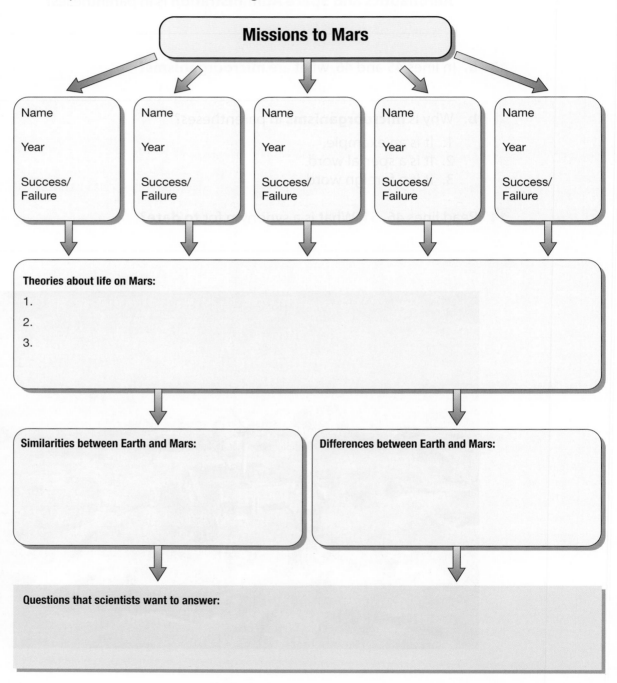

Missions to Mars

Name	Name	Name	Name	Name
Year	Year	Year	Year	Year
Success/Failure	Success/Failure	Success/Failure	Success/Failure	Success/Failure

Theories about life on Mars:

1.

2.

3.

Similarities between Earth and Mars:

Differences between Earth and Mars:

Questions that scientists want to answer:

Information Recall and Summary

Read each question carefully. Use your chart to answer the questions. Do not refer back to the passage. When you are finished, write a brief summary of the reading.

1 What were the names and dates of the missions to Mars? Which ones were successful?

_____

_____

_____

2 Describe the three theories about life on Mars.

a. _____

b. _____

c. _____

3 **a.** How were Earth and Mars similar in the beginning?

_____

_____

_____

_____

_____

b. How did Earth and Mars become different?

_____

_____

_____

4 What do scientists want to learn in the future?

_____

_____

Summary

Work in pairs or alone. Write a brief summary of the reading, and put it on the board. Compare your summary with your classmates'. Which one best describes the main idea of the reading?

_____

_____

_____

E Dictionary Skills

Read the following sentences. Use the context to help you understand the boldface words. Read the dictionary entry for that word and circle the appropriate definition. Then rewrite the sentence, using the definition you have chosen. Be sure to make your sentence grammatically correct.

1 | **perform** _v._ **1** [T] to do or complete a task: _He performed his regular duties quickly and quietly._ **2** [T] to fulfill, satisfy: _The builder performed all the conditions of his contract._ **3** [I] to act, operate, or behave: _She performs well under pressure._ **4** [I; T] to give, act out, or present a performance (of a play, piece of music, dance, etc.): _The actors performed a play for the queen._

In 1976, the _Viking_ spacecraft searched for signs of life, but the tests that [the scientists] **performed** had negative results.

_____

2 | **favorable** _adj._ **1** approving, positive: _I received a favorable report from the doctor._ **2** pleasing: _The first day of class, the instructor made a favorable impression on the students._ **3** advantageous, conducive: _We have favorable weather for our sailing trip now._

Mars also had a thicker atmosphere of carbon dioxide (CO_2). Many scientists think it is possible that life began under these **favorable** conditions.

_____

3 | **condition** *n.* **1** [U] the state of s.t. (good, bad, weak, strong): *The condition of his health is excellent.* || *The condition of that machinery is bad.* **2** [C] a disease, medical problem: *My grandmother has a heart condition.* **3** [C] a requirement: *Our book contract has two special conditions in it; we must pay $10,000 in advance, and we must renew the contract annually.* **4** [C] external factors: *My living conditions were terrible at my old apartment building; I had no running water or heat for two months.* **5** **on the condition that:** provided that: *Yes, we will renew the contract next year on the condition that we make money on the deal.*

They believe that 4.5 billion years ago, Mars and Earth began their existence under similar **conditions.**

F Word Forms

PART 1

In English, some verbs change to nouns in several ways. Some verbs become nouns by adding the suffix –*ion* or –*ation*—for example, *combine (v.)* becomes *combination (n.)*. Complete each sentence with the correct form of the words on the left. **Use the correct tense of the verb in either the affirmative or the negative form. Use the singular or plural form of the noun.**

protect *(v.)*

protection *(n.)*

1. Bicycle helmets _____ cyclists from getting hurt. This kind of _____ is important for both adults and children.

investigate *(v.)*

investigation *(n.)*

2. When the fire started in the house, there was an _____ into how it started. The fire department _____ several different causes.

indicate *(v.)*

indication *(n.)*

3. Very high winds can sometimes _____ a blizzard. There are other _____ as well, such as heavy snow and freezing temperatures.

explore (v.)

exploration (n.)

4 The Viking spacecraft _____ the moon. Instead, its _____ was done on Mars.

combine (v.)

combination (n.)

5 A peanut butter and jelly sandwich is a popular _____ for children. It's so simple that children can _____ the peanut butter and jelly themselves.

PART 2

In English, the verb and noun forms of some words are the same—for example, *travel* (v.) and *travel* (n.). Complete each sentence with the correct form of the words on the left. **Use the correct tense of the verb in either the affirmative or the negative form. Use the singular or plural form of the noun. In addition, indicate whether you are using the noun (n.) or verb (v.) form.**

schedule

1 Debbie has a very busy _____ this semester. She
   (n., v.)

   _____ all of her classes in only 3 days because she
   (n., v.)

   works full time as well.

approach

2 Sophia is very cautious around animals. She _____
   (n., v.)

   a strange dog too quickly. She always takes a slower, more

   careful _____.
   (n., v.)

record

3 Doctors _____ all of their patients' medications on
   (n., v.)

   computers. In this way, they always have a _____ of
   (n., v.)

   their patients' medical histories.

UNIT 4   SCIENCE AND HISTORY

orbit

(4) Each year, the Earth _____ the sun. This complete
    (n., v.)

_____ takes about 12 months.
(n., v.)

map

(5) Carlos needed a _____ to get to a restaurant
    (n., v.)

across town. He couldn't find one, so he used a GPS to

_____ the directions instead.
(n., v.)

Word Partnership	Use *map* with:
adj.	**detailed** map
v.	**draw a** map, **look at a** map, **open a** map, **read a** map

---

G Vocabulary in Context

abundant *(adj.)*	**investigate** *(v.)*	**survive** *(v.)*
arise *(v.)*	**perform** *(v.)*	**theory** *(n.)*
assumption *(n.)*	**similar** *(adj.)*	
intriguing *(adj.)*	**support** *(v.)*	

Read the following sentences. Complete each blank space with the correct word from the list above. Use each word only once.

(1) A human being can _____ without food or water for several

days, but will die within moments without air.

2 The police always _____ murders and robberies to try to find out who committed the crimes so they can arrest them.

3 Water is _____ in many places, but it is rare in deserts.

4 Many scientists have a _____ that some form of life existed on Mars, but to date, there is no proof to support their idea.

5 When Pat opened a letter from the college she had applied to, she began to cry. Susan was watching her and made the _____ that the news was bad. Her guess was correct: Pat was not accepted by the college.

6 Many students do not _____ well on examinations because they become very nervous and tense.

7 Fay suggested a two-month camping trip to the Himalayas next summer. Her husband Luis thought the idea was _____. They had never done anything so exciting before!

8 Venus and Earth are _____ in size. However, the surface temperature of Venus is 600 degrees Fahrenheit!

9 It is probably impossible for life to ever _____ on Venus because of its intense surface heat.

10 Maria will attend college next semester, and her parents agreed to _____ her, so she will not have to get a job.

Critical Thinking Strategies

Read the following questions and think about the answers. Write your answer below each question. Then compare your answers with those of your classmates.

1. "To date, none of the Mars missions has discovered any sure signs of past or present life. Nonetheless, scientists worldwide are not discouraged." Why do you think scientists still believe there might be life on Mars?

   _____

   _____

   _____

2. Scientists' interest in the Red Planet is based on an assumption. Why is there only an assumption? Why can't scientists be sure?

   _____

   _____

   _____

Topics for Discussion and Writing

1. Do you think that life on Earth is simply an accident? Why or why not?

2. Do you think it is important for scientists to study other places in space? Explain your answer.

3. Does your country have a space program? If so, how would you compare it to the space program in the United States?

4. **Write in your journal.** Do you think there is life on another planet? Why or why not?

Follow-Up Activity

Choose a planet in our solar system to read about. Prepare a report on the planet. Use the chart below to record your information. In class, work in groups of three. Discuss the planets you have chosen. Decide whether it is possible for life to exist on these planets. List your reasons. Compare your information with your classmates' information. As a class, decide which planets could possibly support life.

Planet	Diameter and Distance from the Sun	Description of the Planet	Reasons Why Life Is Possible	Reasons Why Life Is Not Possible
Mercury				
Venus				
Earth				
Mars				
Jupiter				
Saturn				
Uranus				
Neptune				

Cloze Quiz

Read the passage below. Fill in the blanks with one word from the list. Use each word only once.

approaches	failed	Martian	spacecraft
combined	failures	missions	success
data	fascinated	neighbor	travel
Earth	information	orbit	unfortunately
exploration	Mars	scientists	unmanned

Ever since people first looked up at the night sky, they have been

_____ by the planet _____. When scientists started using
(1)   (2)

telescopes to try to see the Red Planet, they wondered if there could be life on

Mars. However, for hundreds of years, they could only ask questions. There

was no way to actually _____ to another planet.
(3)

When space _____ began in the 1960s, many countries sent
(4)

_____ spacecraft to Mars to find out everything they could about
(5)

our nearest planetary _____ in space. _____, only half were
(6)   (7)

successful. Twelve _____ landed on the surface, but only seven sent
(8)

_____ back to Earth.
(9)

In spite of the numerous _____, astronomers all over the world
(10)

are hopeful as each Mars mission _____ the Red Planet. For
(11)

example, *Mars Observer*, an American _____, was scheduled to
(12)

move into _____ around Mars and begin sending new information
(13)

back to _____. *Mars Observer* was going to study the _____
(14)   (15)

atmosphere and surface. Unfortunately, _____ lost contact with *Mars*
(16)

Observer, and the mission, which cost $845 million, _____.
(17)

In contrast, the United States' mission to Mars in 1996 was a great

_____. *Mars Pathfinder* sent back more images of Mars than all the
(18)

previous Mars missions _____. More recently, in 2007, the *Mars*
(19)

Reconnaissance Orbiter sent back to Earth more _____.
(20)

Crossword Puzzle

Crossword Puzzle Clues

1. The past tense of **make**
2. Burial place
4. John is sick now, but he will _____ soon.
5. I am; we _____, he is
7. A doctor who performs operations
10. I don't want to study in another country. I need another _____, or choice.
12. I am _____ tired. I slept very well last night.
15. The opposite of **success**
18. The opposite of **difficult**
19. Doubtful; not believing
20. This, that, _____, those
21. You will succeed _____ you work hard.
22. The opposite of **yes**
23. The opposite of **no**
25. An _____ is a person who studies the sun, planets, and stars.
26. Tightly closed
29. Very tired
33. Find
35. To learn very well; to become skilled at something
36. Doctors and nurses care for _____ in hospitals.

1. A simple life form
2. An unproven idea
3. My, his, _____, our, their
6. Dig up
8. Unluckily
9. Not complex
11. The doctor made an _____, or opening, in the patient's chest.
13. Surgery is one kind of medical _____.
14. Researchers perform _____ to test their ideas.
16. An Egyptian king
17. Ask for information
24. Room

27. Required
28. Good, better; bad, _____.
30. The past tense of **have**
31. The opposite of **down**
32. I am going _____ eat lunch.
34. The past tense of **sit**

UNIT 4 | DISCUSSION

1. The three chapters in this unit discuss the uses of technology in solving problems related to the past, the present, and the future. What do you think are the most important problems science and modern technology should try to solve?

_____

_____

_____

_____

_____

2. What can the past teach us about the present? How can this help us in the future?

_____

_____

_____

_____

_____

3. How does technology help us today? Give specific examples.

_____

_____

_____

_____

_____

INDEX OF KEY WORDS AND PHRASES

Words in blue are on the Academic Word List (AWL), Coxhead (2000). The AWL is a list of the 570 highest-frequency academic word families that regularly appear in academic texts. The list was compiled by researcher Averil Coxhead from a corpus of 3.5 million words.

A

absence, 94
abundant, 214
access, 37, 38
according to, 19, 37, 119, 120
accuracy, 137
accurate, 19
accused, 119
adapt, 4
adjusted, 77
affordable, 199
alert, 19
along with, 20
although, 3, 37, 38, 76, 93, 136, 137, 179, 180
altogether, 19
ancient, 179, 180
anesthesiologist, 198
anthropologist, 93, 94
apologized, 3
apparent, 60
apparently, 155
appoint, 119
appropriate, 4
archeologists, 179, 180
arose, 214, 215
arrest, 119, 155
artifacts, 179
as a result, 4, 77, 93, 136, 155, 198
ASL, 59, 60
assumption, 214
astronomers, 214
athletic, 19
atmosphere, 214
attitudes, 19
average, 3, 19
awareness, 19, 20

B

babble, 59, 60
babbling, 59, 60
bail, 119
base, 179
basis, 120
behavior, 3, 4
bitter, 136
blanket, 155
blood, 155
booking, 119
boundless, 37

C

cancer, 198, 199
capacity, 60
carbohydrates, 20
carbon dioxide, 179, 214
case, 119

cell phones, 37, 38
chamber, 179, 180
chance, 93, 94
charges, 119
childhood, 93, 94
cholesterol, 19
chronic, 77, 78
circumstances, 77
civilian, 137
clues, 155, 156
CO_2, 183
common, 76
communicate, 57
communicating, 37
communication, 60
compete, 37, 38
compile, 19
complex, 76, 120, 199, 214
complicated, 4
computer, 37, 155, 198
concern, 37
conditions, 214, 215
confirm, 180
consequence, 19
consequently, 4, 137
consistent, 59
consume, 19, 20
convicted, 119, 136, 137, 155
court, 119, 120, 136, 137
criminal, 119, 136, 155, 156
criminologist, 156
crypt, 179
culture, 4, 19, 93
curtains, 155
custom, 179, 180

D

deaf, 59, 60
decision, 137
decreases, 37
defend, 119
deliberate, 59
despite, 137
devastating, 198
develop, 59, 155, 199, 214, 215
discover, 215
discovered, 3, 94, 137, 215
discovery, 94, 179
disrespectful, 4
double-income, 19
due to, 77, 199

E

e.g., 77
enforcement, 155
enhance, 155
escaped, 179
etc., 3, 77

eventually, 4, 136, 155, 199, 214
evidence, 119, 136, 137, 155, 156, 215
examine, 93, 155, 156, 179
excavation, 179, 180
excited, 37
exclude, 137
exhausted, 198
expensive, 199
expert, 155
extra help, 93
eyewitness, 136, 137

F

fabric, 155
face-to-face, 37
factor, 77, 93, 137
failed, 214
favorable, 214
favorite, 19
few, 3, 94, 155
file, 155
finally, 180
fingerprint, 155
for example, 19, 59, 76, 119, 155, 198, 214
for instance, 60, 77, 137
forensic, 155
furthermore, 37, 137

G

go free, 119
grateful, 199
guilty, 119, 136, 137

H

habits, 19
habitual, 77, 78
harmful, 214
have a break from, 38
hearing, 59, 60, 119
here to stay, 38
household, 94
however, 3, 20, 37, 59, 77, 93, 94, 198, 199, 214

I

if so, 60, 179
ignored, 37
important, 3, 4, 59, 77, 93, 94, 136, 137, 155, 156, 179, 180
improve, 77, 93, 155
in addition, 37, 179
in contrast, 4, 214
in fact, 4, 37, 76, 93, 94, 179, 198
in other words, 60, 77, 93, 119
incision, 198, 199

influence, 93, 137
innate, 60
innocent, 119, 136, 137
in spite of, 214
instantly, 198
instead, 4, 19, 119, 198
intensified, 214
Internet, 37, 38
intriguing, 215
investigate, 180, 214

K
kidney, 198, 199

L
last, 76, 77
lifestyles, 19
linguist, 60
loneliness, 76, 77, 78
lonely, 76, 77, 78

M
mapped, 215
maternal, 94
meaning, 60
medical, 198, 199
memories, 93, 136
microorganisms, 215
microwave, 19
Miranda rights, 119
misinterpret, 4
mission, 214
mistake, 136, 137
mood, 19
moreover, 19
mortality, 93, 94
motions, 59
movements, 59

N
NASA, 215
negative, 214
neither, 4
network, 37
non-destructive, 180
not only . . . but also, 4, 19, 180
numerous, 214
nutrition, 19
nutritional, 20

O
observation, 59
on the average, 19
on the other hand, 3
opening, 198
operating, 198
operation, 198
option, 198
orbit, 214
organisms, 215
otherwise, 119
overcame, 76, 77
ozone, 214

P
parole, 119
paternal, 94

patient, 198
pattern, 19, 59, 60, 155
perform, 214
permanently , 155
pharaoh, 179, 180
phenomenon, 76
plead, 119
popular, 19, 37, 77
population, 94
positive, 136
predict, 76, 179
presence, 93, 94
present, 119, 179, 215
preservation, 179
preserve, 179, 180
prestige, 4
previous, 119, 156, 214
print, 155
privacy, 37
probation, 119
punctual, 3
punishment, 119
purpose, 119

Q
quantity, 19
question, 77

R
rational, 77
react, 3, 198
reasonably sure, 119
records, 19, 94, 119, 155, 215
recover, 179, 198
red meat, 19
Red Planet, 214
reduced, 37, 94, 199
reduction, 37
relax, 38
reliable, 137
remain, 77
require, 76, 156, 198
research, 37
researcher, 37, 76, 77, 179
resolve, 137
respectively, 3
responsibility, 119, 137
restaurateurs, 19
results, 4, 19, 76, 77, 93, 136, 155,
    198, 214
reveal, 155
robot, 198, 199
robotic, 198, 199
role, 93, 94
rude, 3
rush, 20

S
saliva, 155
scene, 155, 156
scent, 179
scientists, 93, 179, 180, 199, 214, 215
sealed, 179, 180
sentencing, 119
serious, 76, 78
severe, 77, 198
shy, 77
significant, 37, 93

similar, 136, 137, 214
site, 180, 215
situational, 76, 77, 78
situations, 19
skeptical, 199
skip, 19
snacks, 19
society, 94
software, 155
solitary, 37
spacecraft, 214, 215
statistics, 19
status, 4
step, 119, 120
surfing, 37
surgeon, 198, 199
surgery, 198, 199
surgical, 198, 199
survey, 19
survive, 93, 214, 215
suspect, 119, 155
sweat, 155, 156
syllable, 60
system, 60, 119, 120, 137, 156, 198, 199

T
technology, 37, 38, 155, 156, 180,
    198, 199
temporary, 76, 78
testified, 136
testimony, 119, 136, 137
theory, 60
thrilled, 37, 215
to date, 215
tomb, 179
traumatic, 198
treatment, 199
treats, 93
trial, 119, 136, 137
tripled, 37
tumor, 199

U
ultraviolet, 214
unacceptable, 4
unfortunately, 77, 214
uniquely, 60
unlike, 77
unlimited, 37

V
value, 137
varied, 59
variety, 20
vibrations, 180
victim, 136

W
while, 3, 4, 20, 37, 78, 156, 214
witness, 119, 136, 137, 155

Y
yet, 136

SKILLS INDEX

GRAMMAR AND USAGE
Cloze quizzes, 16, 34–35, 52–53, 74, 90–91, 111–112, 134, 152–153, 171–172, 194–196, 211–212, 229–230
Word forms
 Adjectives that become nouns by adding -ity, 85–86, 128–129
 Adjectives that become nouns by adding -ness, 84–85
 Adjectives that become nouns by adding -tion or -ation, 46–47
 Adjectives that become nouns by changing final -t to -ce, 68–69
 Adjectives that become nouns by dropping final -t and adding -ce, 103–104
 Adjectives that become verbs by adding -en, 27–28
 Identical noun and verb forms, 45–46, 146–147, 164–165, 206, 224–225
 Verbs that become nouns by adding -ence or -ance, 147–148
 Verbs that become nouns by adding -er, 26–27
 Verbs that become nouns by adding -ing, 69–70
 Verbs that become nouns by adding -ion or -ation, 189, 223–224
 Verbs that become nouns by adding -ment, 129–130, 163, 207
 Verbs that become nouns by adding -tion, 102–103
 Verbs that become nouns by adding -y, 190
 Word order, 8
Word partnerships, 3, 28, 70, 86, 104, 130, 165, 190, 207, 225

LISTENING/SPEAKING
Describing, 15
Discussion, 14, 73, 75, 92, 118, 228
 Topics, 30, 49, 56, 72, 88, 107, 132–133, 150, 167–168, 192–193, 209–210, 227
Group activities, 14, 30, 56, 73, 92, 118, 150–151, 193, 228
Partner activities, 11, 18, 75, 110
Reporting, 154, 211
Role playing, 134, 210
Surveys, 110, 210

READING
Comprehension
 Charts, 31–32, 50–51, 108, 160, 203, 220
 Critical thinking strategies, 30, 48–49, 72, 88, 106–107, 132, 149–150, 167, 192, 209, 227
 Crossword puzzles, 54–56, 113–114, 173–174, 230–232
 Dictionary skills, 25–26, 44, 67, 83–84, 101–102, 126–128, 144–145, 162, 187–188, 205, 222–223
 Fact-finding exercises, 20–21, 38–39, 61, 78–79, 95, 120–121, 138, 157, 181, 200, 216
 Flowcharting, 8, 23, 42, 81, 124
 Follow-up activities, 31–33, 50–51, 73, 89, 108–110, 133–134, 150–151, 168–171, 193, 210–211, 228
 Graphs, 109–110, 169, 170
 Information organization, 8, 23, 42, 64–65, 81, 99, 124, 142, 160, 185, 203, 220
 Information recall and summary, 24, 43, 66, 82–83, 100, 125, 143–144, 160–161, 186–187, 204, 221–222
 Multiple-choice questions, 21–22, 39–41, 50, 62–64, 79–80, 96–98, 108, 121–123, 139–141, 158–159, 169, 170–171, 182–184, 201–203, 217–219
 Outlining, 64–65, 99, 142, 185
 Reading analysis, 21–22, 39–41, 62–64, 79–80, 96–98, 121–123, 139–141, 158–159, 182–184, 201–203, 217–219
 Sentence completion, 13, 108
 Sequencing, 4
 Tables, 75, 76
 True/false questions, 12, 20–21, 38–39, 61, 78–79, 95, 120–121, 138, 157, 181, 200, 216
 Vocabulary in context, 13–14, 28–29, 47–48, 70–71, 86–87, 105–106, 130–131, 148–149, 166–167, 191, 208, 225–226

Group activities, 89
Partner activities, 75, 150–151
Prereading preparation, 18–20, 36–38, 58–60, 75–78, 92–94, 118–120, 135–137, 154–156, 178–180, 197–199, 213–215

TOPICS
A Cultural Difference: Being on Time, 2–17
Ancient Artifacts and Ancient Air, 178–196
Changing Lifestyles and New Eating Habits, 18–35
Innocent until Proven Guilty: The Criminal Court System, 118–134
Language: Is It Always Spoken?, 58–74
Loneliness: How Can We Overcome It?, 75–91
Mars: Our Neighbor in Space, 213–232
Medical Technology: Saving Lives with Robotics, 197–212
Solving Crimes with Modern Technology, 154–175
Technology Competes for Family Time, 36–56
The Importance of Grandmothers, 92–115
The Reliability of Eyewitnesses, 135–153

VIEWING
Charts, 58
Fingerprints, 168–169
Photographs, 9, 36, 118, 135, 168, 197

WRITING
Answers to questions, 24, 30, 31, 32, 43, 66, 72, 76, 82, 88, 100, 106–107, 109–110, 125, 132, 135, 136, 143, 149–150, 160–161, 170, 175, 178–179, 186–187, 197, 204, 209, 210, 221, 227, 232
Charts, 18, 33, 36, 51, 89, 92, 110, 133, 135, 228
Definitions, 58
Description, 18
Explanations, 75
Group activities, 24, 36, 43, 66, 72, 73, 83, 106–107, 132, 135, 144, 149–150, 151, 154, 204, 209, 227, 228
Journals, 15, 30, 49, 72, 88, 107, 133, 150, 168, 193, 210, 227
Lists, 15, 92, 154
Partner activities, 24, 51, 58, 66, 161, 204
Sentences, 9, 19
Summaries, 24, 43, 66, 83, 100, 125, 144, 161, 187, 204, 222
Tables, 151
Topics, 30, 49, 72, 88, 107, 115, 132–133, 150, 167–168, 192–193, 209–210, 227